The Great Britain

K.T.Rowland

THE

GREAT BRITAIN

David & Charles
Newton Abbot

ISBN 0 7153 5160 5

Set in Intertype Baskerville
by Bristol Typesetting Company
and printed in Great Britain
by Redwood Press Limited Trowbridge
for David & Charles (Publishers) Limited
South Devon House Newton Abbot Devon

Contents

List of Illustrations

Author's note

The ss *Great Britain* was and is a unique ship, since she not only played a major part in the transition from sail to steam, but also set the stage for the next century of ship development. Her two major innovations—the use of iron for the hull and screw propulsion—were ultimately adopted as standard practice, although they were challenged by many shipbuilders of the day and for almost a generation afterwards.

Apart from her significance in the evolution of naval architecture, the story of the *Great Britain* provides a fascinating insight to many aspects of mid-Victorian Britain. Her active career from 1844 to 1886 covered a period of consolidation of the Industrial Revolution at home and expansion of British trade and influence overseas. There are today tens of thousands of Australians whose forefathers travelled in her as emigrants. In addition there are the soldiers of famous British regiments whose predecessors sailed in her during her service as a troopship to the Crimea and to India at the time of the Mutiny. The first English cricket team to visit Australia also took passage in her in 1861—this alone might justify her preservation in certain quarters.

I am conscious that in a book of this length I have only been able to cover very briefly the social history of this remarkable ship. Much of the background detail has been obtained from contemporary sources, notably the ship's newspapers written and sometimes printed on board during the long voyages to and from the Antipodes. I have also extracted freely from *The Times* whose correspondents faithfully recorded the highlights of the vessel's early years. For the technical description of the vessel as originally built, I have relied mainly on two sources—the paper presented by Thomas Guppy to the Institution of Civil Engineers in March 1845 and the section relating to the *Great Britain* in *The Life of Isambard Kingdom Brunel*, written by his son and published in 1870. The author had access to many of his father's papers and included as appendices a number of confidential reports made by Brunel to the directors of the Great Western Steamship Company

(GWSC). I have also used the drawings published in 1847 by John
Weale in his book *The Great Britain Atlantic Steam Ship* as a basis
for much of the description of the machinery and hull design. For
information about the stranding at Dundrum Bay I have relied
principally on eye-witness reports in *The Times,* but the description
of the salvage operations conducted by Captain Claxton and James
Bremner has been derived mainly from the correspondence between
Claxton and Brunel which was published in book form in 1847.

I should like to take this opportunity of acknowledging the assistance freely given by the staffs of many libraries and also by
numerous private individuals. In particular I should like to thank
the following organisations for the provision of information and
photographs : Science Museum Library, Westminster Reference
Library, Patent Office Library, The Public Record Office, British
Museum Library, National Maritime Museum, British Rail
Archives, Bristol Reference Library, City Museum Bristol, City of
Liverpool Library, The Mitchell Library, Sydney NSW, Radio
Times Hulton Picture Library, The New Zealand Shipping Co Ltd,
Hopkinson Ltd, San Francisco Maritime Museum and the 'ss Great
Britain Project' Committee. I am especially grateful to Mr Paul W.
Elkin, Curator of Technology at the City Museum Bristol, for the
numerous photographs he provided, several of which showing docu-
ments and drawings were specially taken on my behalf.

In addition I would like to pay tribute to the following private
individuals for their interest and assistance. I should like to thank
Mr Grahame Farr of Bristol whose booklet *The Steamship Great
Britain* issued by the Bristol Branch of the Historical Association
contains a mine of information about the ship. The figures giving
details of the costs of the vessel in Appendix 2 have been reproduced from the above booklet with Mr Farr's kind permission. I am
also grateful to Mr T. P. Langford, also of Bristol, for the details of
the final balance sheet of the GWSC given in Appendix 3. For much
of the information about Captain Gray I am indebted to Captain
Gerald H. Roberts and Captain W. S. Inkster. I should also like to
express my thanks to Mr Bernard Steer, a radio operator in the
Falkland Islands, for permission to quote from his article in the
house journal of the New Zealand Shipping Co Ltd, describing the
condition of the *Great Britain* prior to the salvage operations. Finally
I would like to thank Mr Stephen Green, Curator of the MCC, for
providing various references relating to the Eleven of All England
who travelled to Australia in the ship in 1861.

1 · The Prelude

On 19 July 1843 Bristol was *en fête*. The city had been thronged since the previous evening and hundreds of extra visitors had arrived that morning in early trains from Bath. The church bells rang almost incessantly and saluting guns added to the cacophony of sound at regular intervals—indeed not since the victories of Trafalgar and Waterloo a generation earlier had the citizens of Bristol celebrated with such joyous abandon. The occasion was the launching of the 'great iron ship'—the second vessel to be designed by Isambard Kingdom Brunel for the Bristol-based Great Western Steamship Company.

The celebrations were in a sense an excuse for self-congratulation for this was no ordinary ship but one which had already captured the imagination of the public far beyond the boundaries of Bristol as well as arousing the interest of shipbuilders and marine engineers all over the world. The fact that the *Great Britain* was the largest ship ever built by a comfortable margin, and was also constructed of iron would alone have been sufficient to single her out as a vessel of considerable significance. But she was also the first ocean-going vessel to be fitted with a screw propeller and, in addition, she featured a number of other innovations whose importance was only to be recognised in the years ahead. Probably only a fraction of the crowd who assembled in Bristol that day were directly connected with the fortunes of the *Great Britain* or those of the company which owned her, and yet they came in their thousands, almost as if by premonition, to witness the baptism of a ship that was to set the scene for the next century of ship development.

The launching ceremony was to be performed by His Royal Highness the Prince Consort, an act of royal patronage which was itself indicative of the nation's pride in this latest manifestation of steam power that was revolutionising transport in early Victorian England. Ten years earlier, a visit to Bristol would have entailed a tedious journey by coach with possibly an overnight stop and many intermediate halts for fresh horses; but in 1843, now that Bristol and London were linked by the Great Western Railway (GWR), it was

The launching of the *Great Britain* at Bristol on 19 July 1843. The ship was 'floated out' from the dry dock in which she was built after being named by the Prince Consort

possible to complete the return journey in a single day. The Prince left Buckingham Palace shortly before seven o'clock on the morning of the 19th and was accompanied by the Marquess of Exeter, Mr G. E. Anson and Colonel Beauverie. At Paddington station he was received by a group of directors of the railway company and by Lord Wharncliffe and the Earls of Liverpool and Lincoln. These gentlemen boarded the special train with the Prince which arrived at Temple Meads station, Bristol, at 10 am after a brief stop at Bath. One touch of showmanship, which was perhaps a typical characteristic of the GWR, was that the engine was driven by Daniel Gooch with Brunel himself riding on the footplate in his capacity of chief engineer to the company. The royal party were greeted by the mayor and other civic dignitaries, and the Prince, who wore a plain frock coat with the riband of the Garter, received the

Freedom of the Society of Merchants in a golden casket. No less than sixty local clergymen were also presented personally to the Prince who was afterwards entertained to breakfast by the railway company in the directors' private dining-room before the procession left for the dockyard.

The streets were so packed by this time that the local police found it difficult to manage the crowds and were glad to have the assistance of a detachment of Gloucester police. The procession took a circuitous route eventually crossing Cumberland Basin and driving along Cumberland Road to the works of the GWSC. At the yard the Prince was received by Mr Kingston, the Chairman of the steam-ship company, who introduced him to the other prominent officials. It was now past twelve o'clock and without further delay His Royal Highness walked round the ship in company with Thomas Guppy, the Superintending Engineer. The Royal Standard was broken at the main top as the Prince stepped on board and the colours of the United States, Russia, France and Belgium were hoisted from the other masts. The royal inspection took about two hours and Guppy was called on to explain many details of the construction and design performance of the vessel. A banquet was then held on shore in the vast enginesmith's shop. Over five hundred sat down with Mr Kingston in the chair and the Prince, as the guest of honour, on his right. The American, Prussian and Sardinian Ambassadors were present and various toasts were drunk, but the accompanying speeches must have been commendably brief because it is recorded that the Prince left the improvised banquet room at three o'clock and took his place on the launching platform.

Because of her size the *Great Britain* had been constructed in a specially-built dry dock instead of on a conventional slipway and the launching was to take the form of a ceremonial 'floating out'. She had been built with her bottom above the floor of the dock and the water level had to be pumped above that of the adjacent Floating Harbour before the shores could be removed. By the time the Prince appeared on the scene the waters had been levelled and the dock gates opened. The vessel was riding high in the water since her engines had not yet been installed, although the screw was in position. Her funnel and masts had been temporarily fitted for the occasion and with her glistening new paint she presented a magnificent sight.

The ceremony was watched by vast crowds of people, not only in the immediate vicinity of the dock, but also in vantage points on the other side of the Floating Harbour. On Brandon Hill alone it was estimated that about thirty thousand people assembled and a similar number gathered on the heights of Clifton Wood and on

A poster advertising one of the vantage points for watching the launching ceremony. Thousands flocked to the event—some paid for the privilege but many had a free view

Mardyke Road. Those admitted to the yard had paid 5s for the privilege and were permitted to view from one side of the dock only In addition several hundred more affluent citizens, mainly Bristol merchants and their families, bought tickets for the banquet at 1 gn each which also permitted them to view the ship from all sides and go aboard—a concession which raised loud expressions of discontent from the 5s ticket holders, and the police and yeomanry had to struggle to keep the two parties apart. Unfortunately, this was not the only incident that marred the occasion for the christening ceremony itself hardly went according to plan. Contemporary accounts differ but it appears that the Prince chivalrously invited Mrs Miles, the same lady who had launched the *Great Western* six years earlier, to perform the christening with the traditional bottle of champagne. The steam packet *Avon,* which had been selected to tow the *Great Britain* out of the dock, was too quick off the mark and the great vessel began to move at the same moment as the bottle was released. The cord broke and the bottle, still intact, fell into the water. Prince Albert was equal to the occasion however. Another bottle was obtained and he threw it hard against the iron plates of the ship's side. This time there was no mistake and the bottle smashed into pieces amid tremendous cheers.

An incident such as this at a launch is traditionally considered a bad omen, and since another superstition of the sea had previously been invoked by altering the name of the vessel, not once but twice, there was probably a little apprehension among the more credulous of those present. It is doubtful whether the Prince was concerned since his duty was over, and he had to return to the station to board the special train for London. In the confusion of the christening the tow rope had parted, since the *Avon* had moved off before all the shores had been removed. It took some time before this could be connected again, and the operation of moving the vessel into the Floating Harbour took place after the Prince had left for London.

Thus ended the most publicised, if not the most spectacular, ship launching that was to occur in Victorian England until that of the *Great Eastern* some fifteen years hence. No doubt the directors of the company were gratified by the tremendous public interest which promised well for future bookings, and all connected with the vessel must have been relieved that after four years of labour, her final completion date could be predicted with reasonable confidence.

There is no record of Brunel's feelings on this day of triumph. He was normally indifferent to public opinion as far as his professional work was concerned, but from his correspondence with his associates on the building committee, it is clear that he was aware that his reputation was at stake and that the *Great Britain* represented a step into the unknown to a greater extent than anything he had undertaken previously. In 1843, Brunel was in his thirty-seventh year, yet he had already accomplished more than most engineers could hope to achieve in one, or even several, life spans. In an age of great practical innovators he was outstanding, and his versatility was such that he had already made major contributions to all the principal branches of engineering science. Unlike many of his contemporaries, he had not risen from the ranks of the millwrights, but was the son of an equally illustrous father, Marc Brunel. His father was an *emigré* Frenchman who at one time had been Chief Engineer to the City of New York before his patented machine for making ships' blocks had led to his permanent domicile in England. Between 1799 and 1825 he took out no less than eighteen British patents covering machines concerning copying, shoe manufacture, printing, steam power, tunnelling and other totally unrelated subjects. Isambard Brunel obviously inherited his father's flair and versatility, although he himself never took out a single patent during his lifetime. He was, in fact, a staunch opponent of the patent laws which he regarded as an impediment to the advance of technology.

Isambard Kingdom Brunel,
designer of the *Great Britain*

Brunel's education had been thorough but hardly conventional. He spent some time at a private school in Brighton and then moved to the college of Henri Quatre in Paris where he excelled at mathematics and drawing. Instead of entering a university he joined his father's office in 1823, where he soon showed a precocious talent for tackling the almost insoluble problems associated with the building of the first tunnel under the Thames. His association with Bristol began in 1829, when his design was accepted for a suspension bridge over the Avon Gorge at Clifton. He was afterwards appointed Engineer of Bristol Docks where his work brought him into contact with many prominent merchants in the city. At the age of twenty-seven in 1833, he was appointed Engineer to the newly formed GWR and began his monumental construction of the line from London to Bristol. This was much bolder in conception than anything undertaken elsewhere in the genesis of railway engineering, and the viaducts, bridges and tunnels are to this day among Brunel's lasting memorials.

It was at a meeting of the GWR in October 1935 at Radley's Hotel, Blackfriars that one of the directors expressed his misgivings about the enormous length of the main line that the company was constructing. Brunel then made his famous remark suggesting that the railway should be extended to New York by means of a steamship service plying between Bristol and the New World. This was contrary to all established thinking in shipping circles of the day, where it was predicted that if a regular transatlantic steam service ever became a reality, it would have to operate on the European side from the farthermost ports in the south-west of Ireland.

Brunel's remarks however were taken up by Thomas Guppy, one of the four British merchants who had originated the project of a railway. Later that evening Guppy and three fellow directors, Scott, Pycroft and Bright, discussed the proposal enthusiastically with Brunel. The result was the formation of the GWSC in January 1836. A prospectus was issued with a capital of £250,000 which was quickly subscribed and offices were opened at 35 Prince Street, Bristol. The promoters of the company were chiefly GWR directors (whose names are starred) and the original board was made up as follows :

DIRECTORS : P. Maze* (Chairman), R. Bright,* H. Bush, H. Godwin, T. R. Guppy,* T. Kingston, R. Scott,* T. B. Were, C. Claxton.

TRUSTEES : J. Coolson, J. Harford,* T. Kingsbury, J. Vining.*

AUDITORS : C. B. Fripp, J. Winwood, J. Mexham.

The most significant appointment was that of I. K. Brunel as chief engineer.

To assess objectively Brunel's contribution to the development of steam navigation, it is necessary to consider the progress achieved up to the formation of the GWSC. Regular scheduled passenger services across the Atlantic had been in existence since 1816, but they were maintained by sailing vessels and were dominated by American companies operating out of New York and Boston. The first on the scene had been the celebrated Black Ball Line and this was followed by the Swallow Tail, Red Star, Black Star, Black X and White Diamond Lines, who all conducted their business in fierce competition with one another. Their vessels—mainly between three and five hundred tons—were the forerunners of the magnificent clipper ships of the 1860s. They had excellent sailing qualities and could maintain 12–14 knots under favourable conditions. A good time for a west-east passage was about twenty-three days while the return journey against the prevailing westerlies might take up to forty days. British shipowners and builders were protected to a certain extent by the Navigation Laws in force at the time but they had no effective answer to their transatlantic rivals. And unlike their counterparts on the New England coast, British shipbuilders were handicapped by the scarcity and rising price of suitable timber. This was to have far reaching consequences, and was one of the factors which precipitated the use of iron in British shipyards.

America had also led the way in establishing the first successful steamboat services in the rivers and along the coastal stretches of the Eastern seaboard. Following the pioneering work of men such as John Fitch and James Rumsey, Robert Fulton introduced the first profitable steamboat service on the Hudson river in 1807. It is true that the engine of the *Clermont*, Fulton's first successful steamboat, came from the Soho Foundry of Boulton & Watt, but within a few short years vessels fitted with American-built machinery were in the service of the numerous steamship companies that proliferated between Maine and the Carolinas during the immediate pre-railway period. Development proceeded rapidly, and as early as 1815, Fulton designed the twin-funnelled *Chancellor Livingston* for the Albany-New York service, with berths for 120 passengers and standing room for many more—the journey being covered at an average speed of 9 knots.

The first successful commercial service in Britain was inaugurated by Henry Bell's *Comet* on the Clyde in 1812. Although other small steamboats soon appeared on the Thames, Mersey and the other principal rivers, it was many years before a vessel comparable to the *Chancellor Livingston* was built. There were several reasons for initial American pre-eminence, but primarily the topography of the original thirteen states, where more natural barriers existed, ensured a greater chance of operating a profitable service than in the countries of the Old World where shorter distances favoured the already established turnpike and canal systems. It was hardly surprising therefore, that the first steamship to cross the Atlantic was also American-built. The voyage of the *Savannah* in 1819 was however a commercial failure, and the vessel spent only about eighty-five hours under steam during her passage of $27\frac{1}{2}$ days from Savannah, Georgia to Liverpool.

During the 1820s, several steamships built in British and Continental yards made the passage in both directions, but again most of the journey was under sail. With the low boiler pressures and uneconomical single expansion engines of the day, the fuel consumption per indicated horse power was so great that their range under steam was severely limited. Circumstances began however to work in favour of British shipbuilders as the Industrial Revolution gained momentum, and a number of important engine building companies

William Patterson, from an early photograph probably taken during the eighteen forties

were formed. Among these were those of Maudslay Sons and Field, John Penn & Sons, Seaward Brothers and Miller & Barnes on the Thames, and the companies set up by David and Robert Napier on Clydeside. Under the impetus of this expansion, engine design gradually improved, although working steam pressures remained woefully inadequate. Nonetheless, the introduction of new and improved machine tools and a better understanding of materials made it possible for the engine builders to increase the size of their engines, and consequently their power output until, by 1836, engines developing between two and three hundred ihp were not uncommon.

These developments had not escaped the notice of the more enterprising and perceptive individuals in the shipping industry, and in 1833, two years before the fateful meeting in Radley's Hotel, Robert Napier had been asked to report on the prospects of a regular transatlantic steam service. Napier was the son of a Dumbarton blacksmith, who by 1830 had become one of the leading marine engine builders in Britain. Unlike many of his London competitors, who were able to secure lucrative Admiralty contracts, most of Napier's early work concerned passenger ships serving the short sea-routes around the British Isles. Given his connections with the merchant service, it was natural that his advice should be sought on what should prove to be the most profitable steamship route of all. Napier, the cautious Scot, was in favour of the project provided that specially-built vessels were employed. He insisted that they should be equipped with spare gear in order that any components failing during the voyage could be replaced, and that no expense should be spared on the materials used for the engines and boilers. He also stipulated that engineroom crew should be hand-picked by the chief engineer, and that they should all be tradesmen. In conclusion he reported to the effect that if steam vessels were able to make a few quick trips and beat sailing vessels decisively, then the battle would be won and the field would belong to the protagonists of steam.

This was exactly what the more adventurous spirits in the shipping world wanted to hear. But there were others who argued that it was beyond the capacity of any steamship likely to be built in the foreseeable future. They reasoned that, if the size of the hull was doubled in order to increase the coal carrying capacity, the ship would require double the power to drive it. Coal consumption would be doubled and therefore, no matter how large a vessel was built, it would still consume all its fuel before it could complete the journey. Those who opposed these views put forward the simple but obvious formula that while the carrying capacity of the hull increased as the cube of its dimensions, its resistance, or the power required to drive it through the water, increased only as the square of those dimensions. Among the firmest advocates of the latter point of view were Brunel and the directors of the GWSC, and it was only to be expected that such a group of able and determined entrepreneurs would not regard the problem as merely an academic exercise. This was confirmed in June 1836 when the keel of the company's first ship, the *Great Western,* was laid down at Bristol in the Wapping Yard of William Patterson.

Although Brunel had never designed a ship before, his thorough understanding of materials and appreciation of the basic forces involved led him to adopt a most satisfactory solution for the hull design. He realised that to resist the continuous buffeting of the heavy Atlantic waves great longitudinal strength was necessary, and although the vessel was timber-built her bottom frames were reinforced by four staggered rows of 24in long iron bolts which ran the entire length of the ship. The ribs were of oak and of scantling equal to the ships of the line of the day. Another similarity to naval construction was the copper sheathing of the hull below the waterline. The choice of machinery was obviously a critical factor, as the success of the venture would depend on attaining a maximum power/fuel consumption factor. Several firms tendered for this contract, but on Brunel's advice the order was awarded to the Lambeth engineers, Maudslay Sons and Field. The engines, the largest the company had ever built, were of a standard side-lever design. This type of engine was a direct development of Watt's beam engine in which the single overhead beam was replaced by two levers, one on either side of the cylinder. This arrangement saved a considerable amount of headroom and improved stability. In the *Great Western* there were two 73.5in diameter cylinders and the length of the piston stroke was 7ft. Steam was supplied at 5lb per sq in from four iron return-flue boilers, each having three furnaces. The total power indicated by the engines was 750 ihp, a figure appreciably greater than anything previously attained.

Nevertheless, the machinery of the *Great Western* was to exhibit one serious defect which only became apparent after the vessel had been in service for a period. Her coal consumption was still enormous in relation to her size and a large proportion of the available cargo space had to be devoted to the coal bunkers which had a serious effect on profitability. This subsequently had an important bearing on the size of hull selected for the *Great Britain* as Brunel was to recognise, that with the inefficient steam engines of the day operating on low pressure steam, it would be necessary to increase the size of ships to make them competitive on the Atlantic route.

In 1837 however, when the *Great Western* was launched, this problem was not foreseen and once it was realised in shipping circles that the *Great Western* might well succeed in her purpose and would then have an unchallenged monopoly, other companies were quickly formed to compete on the route. The first two serious rivals were the British and American Steam Navigation Company of London and the Transatlantic Steamship Company of Liverpool. Both these companies immediately laid down vessels that were comparable in size to the *Great Western,* but then realising that the lead of Patterson's yard at Bristol was too great, they decided to charter vessels in an effort to make the first crossing.

The final stages of fitting out the *Great Western* took place in the Thames where the engines were installed by Maudslays. Trials were held at the end of March 1838, but on the 28th of that month the *Sirius,* which had been chartered by the British and American Steam Navigation Company, set sail from London for New York. The *Sirius* had been built for service between London and Cork. She was much smaller than the *Great Western,* her gross registered tonnage being only 703 tons against 1320 of Brunel's vessel. But her coal consumption was disproportionately high, being 80 per cent that of the *Great Western* while her size and bunker capacity was roughly half. As experience was to show, she was in no way equipped to maintain a sustained service across the North Atlantic, but she had one decisive advantage in the race to New York—simply that she was ready first by a margin of about five days. The trials of the *Great Western* were satisfactory, but a small fire in the boiler room occurred when the vessel left Gravesend for Bristol on 31 March, which resulted in a delay of 12 hours and caused fifty out of the fifty-seven passengers who had booked for the voyage to cancel their passages. This was not an auspicious start to the company's first venture and the chance of the *Great Western* overhauling the *Sirius* seemed slight when she finally left Bristol on Sunday 8 April after taking on coal and stores. Because of her shorter range the *Sirius* had to coal ship again at Cork, and she subsequently encountered strong headwinds in mid-Atlantic which affected her speed more than her more robustly built rival. The *Great Western* steadily closed the gap, but in the end she had to concede victory by a few hours. Both ships were greeted with great enthusiasm by huge crowds on arrival in New York, but it was the feat of Brunel's vessel that aroused the interest of the more perceptive American observers, especially when it became known that 200 tons of coal were left in the bunkers after steaming continuously for 15 days 5 hours at an average speed of 8.8 knots. The era of rapid and reliable ocean transport was at hand and the American hegemony of the North Atlantic was no longer unchallenged.

2 · Building the Great Britain

On the return voyage, her first eastbound crossing, the *Great Western* carried sixty-eight passengers in contrast to the intrepid seven who had been aboard for the maiden voyage to New York. After another triumphant reception at Bristol she resumed her role as the first successful steamship constructed specifically for the North Atlantic service. She continued to ply between Bristol and New York, and altogether made the crossing sixty-four times during the eight years between 1838 and 1846.

The directors of the GWSC soon appreciated that more than one vessel was required to sustain a successful service, and in the late summer of 1838 it was announced that another ship would be built of equal size to the *Great Western* and that she would be called the *City of New York*. Obviously the astute Bristol merchants were already aware of the importance of attracting American passengers. The original plans were for a wooden vessel driven by paddles—the conventional form of construction of the day. A cargo of African oak timber was purchased which was sufficient for the new vessel and others of similar size.

The question of the most suitable size was undoubtedly critical and it was reasoned that the advantages gained by the *Great Western* over the *Sirius* and her contemporaries would be magnified if a ship of even greater dimensions was constructed. Soon there was general agreement that a vessel of not less than 2000 tons gross weight would be necessary, which was half as large again as the *Great Western*.

It was not until October 1838, however, that the first radical alteration was proposed. Thomas Guppy communicated to the Board the results of calculations made by Brunel regarding the comparable merits of iron and timber as materials for hull construction. Experience in the use of iron was still scanty and Brunel suggested that Captain Claxton RN, one of the principal directors, and William Patterson, the builder of the *Great Western*, should obtain first hand information on the behaviour of iron steamships by taking a passage to Antwerp and back in the *Rainbow*, a small paddle steamer of 407 tons burden which had been built by John Laird of Birkenhead in the previous year. Both were impressed by the performance of the *Rainbow* and a report was prepared which was strongly in favour of the adoption of iron. There is no indication when the decision was taken by the Board, although a note appeared in a Bristol newspaper on 30 March 1839 of a rumour to this effect. The significance of this decision, which was to lead to a major advance in the development of shipbuilding, can only be fully appreciated when the progress made in the use of iron up to 1839 is considered. For at that time there was still considerable opposition to its adoption by almost every section of the shipping industry—not least being that insurance underwriters were liable to charge higher premiums for insuring iron ships.

Experience in the use of iron for vessels of all types dated from the last quarter of the eighteenth century when John Wilkinson of Bradley Forge built a canal barge using 15 cwt of iron plates which were approximately $\frac{5}{16}$in thick. The first recorded use of iron for a craft operating in sea water occurred in August 1815 when Thomas Jevons launched a small iron boat on the tidal reaches of the Mersey. This was built by Joshua Horton at Tipton, Staffordshire but fitted out at Liverpool by Roger Hunter and F. J. Humble. The little craft, which was used as a pleasure boat, was reported to have excellent sailing qualities but it disappeared from its moorings without trace one night and was afterwards discovered at the bottom of Duke's Dock. Jevons attributed the accident to malicious damage by persons unknown. In 1818 he lodged a *Caveat* at the Patent Office with a view to taking out a patent on iron boats. His interests were directed towards the use of iron for lifeboats and an example of this type of vessel was built for him by Joshua Horton.

The first iron steamship was constructed by another Tipton man, Aaron Manby, and it seems fair to assume that Manby was influenced or at least was aware of the smaller vessels built by Horton. Manby was the owner of the Horsley Ironworks near Tipton and in 1821 he took out patent No 4558 for an oscillating steam engine which was one of the first of several patents to be granted for this type. In the following year he began constructing an iron ship in which he intended to install the engine. The hull was fabricated at Manby's works and then transported in sections to the Surrey Docks at Rotherhithe where it was assembled. The vessel was named after her owner—*Aaron Manby;* her principal dimensions were length 106.8ft, beam 17.2ft, draught 3.5ft and the burden was 116 tons. Steam was supplied by two flat-sided iron boilers at 2lb per sq in and her top speed was 7 knots. Trials were successfully held on the Thames in May 1822, and Manby then dispatched the craft from

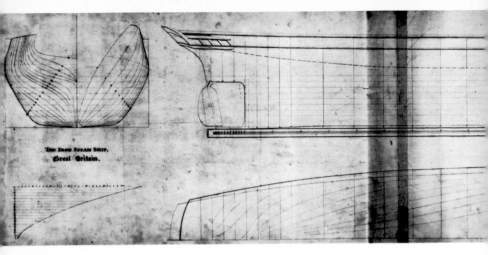

The hull design which was largely the work of William Patterson

London direct to Le Havre with a cargo of linseed and iron castings. The vessel was under the command of Charles Napier, a friend of Manby's who afterwards became Admiral Sir Charles Napier RN and a leading advocate of the 'steam and iron' navy which was eventually to displace the wooden walls of England.

For several years Manby was to remain the only builder of iron ships. There was inherent resistance to an innovation which cut right across established shipbuilding techniques and, in fact, demanded less of the old-established skills of the carpenters and shipwrights. Nevertheless, the production of wrought iron in Britain was increasing rapidly and the price of iron plate began to decrease while timber was becoming scarcer and dearer, so that economic considerations, if nothing else, began to favour the use of iron.

Other engineers and shipbuilders began to argue the case for iron ships as experience of their use in service accumulated. Among these were men such as William Fairburn, John Grantham, Charles Williams, the Managing Director of the City of Dublin Steam Packet Company, and the Liverpool shipbuilders Macregor and John Laird. It was John Laird who became the principal builder of iron ships in the 1830s and who, in 1834, built the steamship *Garry Owen* for service on the lower reaches of the River Shannon. This little paddle steamer of 263 tons burden was to occupy an important place in the development of shipbuilding. She was driven ashore in a violent gale but was saved from breaking up by her iron construction. Charles Williams was consultant to the owners of the *Garry Owen* and he is alleged to have first introduced the use of watertight bulkheads in this vessel, although this advance has been generally attributed to Brunel. It is certain that Williams never took out a patent, although he did patent several inventions relating

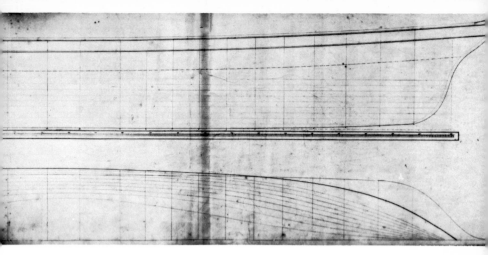

to boilers and furnaces in the years between 1839 and 1842. The performance of the *Garry Owen* helped above all to establish public confidence in the seaworthiness of iron ships and led John Laird, in 1837, to build the *Rainbow,* which was to be examined so carefully by Brunel and his colleagues.

When the decision was taken on the advice of Brunel to use iron for a ship to follow the *Great Western,* there was little more than fifteen years' service experience with that material, and the largest vessel up to that time was hardly a quarter of the size of the proposed new ship. When examined in this context, Brunel's flair for innovation and bold self-confidence becomes apparent. His decision to recommend iron was not, of course, based on commercial considerations alone. He possessed a thorough understanding of the material and of the forces involved, and the experience that he had acquired with the Great Western Railway was to be invaluable.

It has already been noted that the economic advantages of iron over timber were beginning to be appreciated towards the end of the 1830s especially as timber ships often required expensive copper sheathing below the waterline to prevent the ravages of toredo worms and other marine borers. John Grantham, who wrote one of the earliest books (1842) on the use of iron in shipbuilding, suggested that apart from the cost of the copper sheathing there was little difference between iron and timber for vessels below 300 tons. Above this figure iron was cheaper than timber, and for really large merchant ships and warships iron was much less expensive. Grantham also pointed out that the stowage space in an iron ship was greater than one of timber with identical external dimensions. This was because the shell of a timber vessel was much thicker and on a ship the size of the *Great Britain* it was estimated that there would be a gain of 20 per cent more cargo space in the hold by using iron.

Iron as a material also gave the shipbuilder more scope in the design of the hull, although most of these benefits were not to be realised until after the work of William Froude later in the century. Undoubtedly the finer lines that were possible with iron eventually helped to increase speeds although the *Great Britain* was to be marginally slower than most of her contemporaries when she was launched. There can be no doubt however that Patterson, who was responsible for the hull design, achieved a combination of grace and strength that established the pattern for others to follow as iron ships became more popular.

The preparation of the design of the new vessel, still known officially as the *City of New York,* took some time and no less than five sets of drawings were produced. The vessel grew in size with each alteration until eventually the burden was 3443 tons. At about this time her name was changed appropriately to the *Mammoth.* Local shipbuilders were invited to tender but because of the size and many innovations in the design they declined. No doubt the fact that the hull was to be built of iron helped to influence their decision, particularly in view of the special equipment that was required. The company therefore decided to build the vessel themselves, and purchased a site at the lower end of Wapping Wharf between the present Cumberland Road and the Floating Harbour. A dry dock was excavated since it was considered that a vessel of the proposed size would be difficult to control if launched from a slipway in the conventional manner. The dock was sited at an angle to facilitate the floating out operation, confidently expected to be only a year or so ahead. The works were built adjacent to the dock and equipped as quickly as possible with all the tools and machines necessary for the construction of iron ships. These included machines for shearing and punching plates, bending machines, drilling and countersinking machines and furnaces for heating plates and rivets. The cost of the completed works was £53,000. With a sense of urgency, which was characteristic of Brunel and the GWR, two hundred gas burners were provided so that work could proceed in the hours of darkness. The dock was originally known as the Great Western Dock, although the name was subsequently changed to the Wapping Dry Dock.

The company was not idle while the works were being constructed and sub-contracts were negotiated for special items of equipment. The *Railway Magazine* of 1839 reported that the local Bristol foundry of Bush & Beddoes had made an open-cast oblong plate measuring 17ft 6in by 7ft 6in and 3in thick for the purpose of bending iron plates. The casting weighed between 5 and 6 tons and contained 2236 cores or holes and 48 countersunk holes. The equipment was described simply as being for the 'iron ship' which is an indication probably of the writer's confusion over the name of the vessel that was soon to be changed for the second and last time to *Great Britain*.

Invitations to tender for the engines had been sent out as early as November 1838 to three companies, namely Maudslays Sons and Field, Seaward Brothers and Halls of Dartford. At that time it was thought that sufficient power to drive conventional paddles could be supplied by a unit having two cylinders of 88in diameter. Maudslays, who had supplied the engines for the *Great Western,* originally declined to tender and negotiations were broken off as it became apparent that even larger engines would be required as the size of the vessel increased with each successive set of plans. In April 1839, estimates for engines having cylinders of 100in diameter and a 7ft stroke were sought from several leading manufacturers. Maudslays submitted proposals on this occasion and after due deliberation it was clear to the building committee of Brunel, Guppy and Captain Claxton that the choice lay between Maudslays' design and a trunk engine which had been patented by a young engineer named Francis Humphys. Brunel, who favoured Maudslays and thought that Humphys' estimate was over sanguine, requested that both

The Great Western Dry Dock, Bristol—sometimes known as the Wapping Dry Dock. It was in this dock that the *Great Britain* was built in 1839–44 and it was to this dock that the vessel returned in July 1970

parties should prepare further tenders for engines with cylinders of 120in diameter. He asked the directors to postpone their decision until Maudslays had the necessary time to develop their new double cylinder or 'Siamese' engine which had recently been patented. The directors however were anxious to proceed without further delay and Brunel was asked by Maze, the chairman, to submit a report on the tenders, which he did in writing to the board on 12 June 1839.

Humphys' estimate was the lower by a considerable margin and, even with additional modifications recommended by Brunel and Guppy, amounted only to £30,700. The design was for a twin cylinder engine with cylinders of 110in diameter and a stroke of 8ft. The principal drawback, which weighed against immediate acceptance, was that the company would have to build the engines themselves since Halls of Dartford, who held the manufacturing rights, were not prepared to tool up for a contract involving only a single pair of engines.

Maudslays' final tender was for an engine of four 75in cylinders. The total cost was estimated at £41,150, with an additional charge of £2000 for freight and insurance to cover the journey from the engine works at Lambeth to Bristol and installation in the ship. Brunel recognised the merits of both designs, but he questioned the wisdom of the company undertaking additional manufacturing obligations when they were already committed to building a ship more than twice the size of any that had hitherto been launched. In his opinion, the extra costs of tooling and building the necessary engine shops would exceed the difference between the tenders. Furthermore, he pointed out that the Maudslay design included such refinements as the recently patented Kingston non-return valves, and apparatus for changing the water in the boiler which had been invented by Joshua Field. And while Brunel was of the opinion that the company would, in time to come, have to build their own engines, he advised that this step should be delayed until a third vessel was built. The directors decided however, that the acquisition of an engine shop and the associated equipment would be a valuable asset, and that they should take advantage of Humphys' lower tender.

In retrospect it would appear that the company's fortunes started to wane when they decided to build the *Great Britain* themselves and incurred the further liability of becoming engine builders as well. The *Great Britain* is probably the only major vessel to have been constructed, fitted with engines and operated by the same company. This policy of self-sufficiency had been pursued successfully by the Great Western Railway and its contemporaries, but while it could be applied to what was essentially a new form of transport, it was impossible for a company without previous experience to build a ship and assume the responsibility for all her internal machinery without incurring grievous financial penalties, even if they succeeded magnificently in overcoming the technical problems.

As soon as the directors had made their decision, work was put in hand to add the additional workshops and equipment; and Francis Humphys was appointed as the engineer-in-charge. It was obvious from the beginning that the tremendous size of the cylinders and crankshaft was going to present some monumental problems. For although the development of improved casting and machining techniques had made rapid progress during the previous quarter of a century the task, for example, of casting and machining accurately two cylinders, each having a diameter of 110in, would be no mean accomplishment. Very large cylinders had, of course, been produced for 'Newcomen' or atmospheric pumping engines for some years, but these did not require such fine tolerances as a condensing engine in which the steam was to work expansively.

Humphys' engine was described as a trunk engine. Patent No 6801 was granted to him on the 28 March 1835 for a marine steam engine in which the movement of the piston was transmitted to the crank without the intervention of 'beams, crossheads and other auxiliary appendages in common use'. The essence of the patent was the provision of a steamtight casing or trunk which was permanently attached to the piston and moved up and down with it. The stuffing box was arranged to fit the trunk instead of the pistol rod. The latter, which was attached to the lower side of the piston, passed through the trunk and was connected directly to the crank. The trunk itself had to be accurately machined, ground and polished, and the cylinder cover had also to be a very good fit. The stuffing box was packed with either metallic packing or hemp, flax or cotton. It was also steam packed to prevent air from entering the cylinder rather in the manner of a modern low pressure turbine gland. The design had certain merits in that it reduced the number of moving parts and its relative simplicity meant a decrease in size and weight of the principal components, and hence less wear and tear. In addition, it was another attempt to solve one of the major problems that confronted the early marine engine designers, since it reduced the height of the engine, increased stability by lowering the centre of gravity and made possible the location of a larger and more powerful unit within the same space between decks.

Although the casting of the cylinders and the subsequent boring operations demanded a high degree of accuracy it was the construction of the massive paddle shaft which was to present the most difficult problem. The shaft was so large that there was not a hammer in the country capable of forging it and Humphys, after a fruitless search, even considered using cast iron. All the heavy forging work at that time was performed by tilt hammers which had hardly changed in design for more than two hundred years. Humphys eventually approached James Nasmyth, a former pupil of Henry Maudslay, who was then a partner in the firm of Nasmyth, Wilson and Company. Nasmyth's solution was to design the world's first steam hammer, an invention which was comparable in importance with the screw-cutting lathe in the history of machine tool development. Nasmyth's hammer accomplished the task for which it had been designed but the massive paddle shaft was destined never to be used. It was rendered obsolete almost as soon as it had been finished by Brunel's decision to use the screw propeller.

Like all truly successful innovators, Brunel had the capacity of selecting able subordinates and then delegating to them a considerable degree of responsibility. He arranged for one of his assistants, Berkeley Claxton, to make six voyages in the *Great Western* to obtain data relating to rolling and pitching, and to study the performance of the engines with particular reference to the use of the expansion valves. The high coal consumption of early marine engines was always a major problem, and the use of steam expansively by cutting off its admission to the cylinder, when only part of the inlet stroke was completed, offered significant economies. Brunel at this time was obviously reappraising the basic design of the vessel including the means of driving the ship through the water. The information collected by Berkeley Claxton led him to doubt the efficiency of the paddle system and when, early in 1840, an experimental steamer equipped with a screw propeller arrived in Bristol, he decided to investigate the merits of this novel method of propulsion.

The selection of iron had indeed been a bold step, but the subsequent adoption of the screw propeller made the *Great Britain* a vessel of unique importance and the true forerunner of practically every ship on the high seas today—130 years after Brunel's inspired decision. In 1840, there was hardly any experience of marine propellers in service, and Brunel with his customary thoroughness decided that a period of trial and observation would be necessary before an irrevocable step was taken. The vessel which had visited Bristol was the *Archimedes,* a three-masted topsail schooner of 237 tons burden. She was owned by the Ship Propeller Company and was fitted with a screw propeller designed by Francis Pettit Smith whose patent the company had purchased. Smith was only one of a number of enterprising inventors who had proposed the use of a screw for ships' propulsion although, apart from John Ericsson, the celebrated Swedish engineer, he probably made a greater contribution and was rewarded with greater commercial success than most of his rivals. The first man to consider driving a screw with a steam engine was Joseph Bramah in 1785, but there is no record that this was ever put into effect. Between 1785 and 1836, when Smith's patent was granted, a number of other inventors appeared on the scene, but their practical success was small apart from that of Bennett Woodroft, whose first propeller patent was taken out in 1832. This was afterwards renewed in the 1840s following long and costly litigation after which many of the minor patentees withdrew.

For many years after screw propulsion was introduced, there was no definitive propeller design which would unquestionably yield the best results. This is obvious by the number of different propellers that were fitted and by the empirical approach employed by all shipbuilders until theoretical data became available to designers. The *Archimedes* herself was no exception, and several different screws of Smith's design were used even before her visit to Bristol.

Thomas Guppy, whose energy and resourcefulness made him an invaluable member of the building committee, played an important part in the events which were to lead to the adoption of screw propulsion. He was one of a party of directors of the company who made an excursion to the Holms 30 miles from Bristol in the *Archimedes* at the invitation of her owners. He was so impressed with the performance of the screw that he arranged to make a longer voyage to Liverpool. On the passage up the Irish Sea rough weather was encountered, and Guppy was able to observe the screw under adverse as well as favourable conditions. On his return to Bristol he reported to the building committee and on Brunel's advice the directors ordered work on the paddle engines to cease for three months while the advantages claimed for the screw were further evaluated.

Brunel's report was submitted in October 1840. It was a document of about ten thousand words which compared in detail the performance of the *Archimedes* with that of the *Great Western*. In his summary he listed impartially the merits and defects of screw propulsion. The screw was not so accessible, it required a vessel of a particular form and it was liable to lift out of the water when the ship pitched in rough weather. The major problem was the need to step up the engine revolutions by means of gearing or a similar device and it is apparent that Brunel considered that the solution chosen in the *Archimedes* caused unnecessary vibration. He favoured the use of straps instead of gearing, and this was the means eventually adopted, although the straps were replaced by chains.

Experiments were carried out in the company's works under Brunel's supervision, using special hemp straps, proving that this approach was feasible and that the straps would not stretch and slip in service.

Once he was satisfied that the gearing problem could be overcome Brunel had no doubts about the potential superiority of the screw. He put forward six principal advantages. Firstly, there would be a considerable saving in weight and this would be mainly top weight. Altogether he calculated that there would be an overall decrease of about 95 tons. Secondly, the elimination of paddleboxes simplified construction, saved a considerable amount of money and enabled the lines of the ship to be preserved thus offering less resistance to head winds and through the water. Furthermore, the screw, being positioned on the centreline of the ship, was not affected by rolling. This was one of the serious disadvantages of paddles since their efficient action depended on maintaining a constant depth of immersion. The provision of a screw also permitted free use of sails since the screw could be uncoupled and if necessary raised out of the water. This was perhaps a negative advantage but it was a true prediction of developments in the immediate future when the use of sails was obligatory on voyages to Australia and the Far East because of the tremendous coal consumption of the single expansion engines. The superior performance of a screw in a beam sea would mean a more regular motion of the shaft and less chance of a violent shock being transmitted to the engines as was often the case when paddlewheels were alternatively immersed and lifted clear of the water. Another advantage suggested by Brunel was that since the thrust of the screw impinged directly on the rudder, which was situated immediately astern, there would be greater response to movement of the rudder. This would be due to the mass of water through which the rudder was moving having a greater velocity than the ship herself. Finally there was the decrease in the beam of the vessel. This had special significance in Brunel's view because of the circumstances peculiar to Bristol, where the narrow openings of the lock gates would prevent large vessels from using the City Docks. The breadth across the paddleboxes, as originally planned, was 78ft but this would be reduced to nearer 50ft by eliminating the paddles. Brunel, in fact, was showing more foresight than he probably realised at the time and had the original plans not been altered the difficulties, which were later experienced when the *Great Britain* finally moved out of the Float, would have been magnified a hundredfold.

The directors were impressed by the arguments put forward by their chief engineer and screw propulsion was accordingly adopted, thus ensuring lasting fame for their vessel, although she was hardly off the drawing board. The form which the screw should take remained to be decided and further trials were held with the *Archimedes*, the vessel being lent by The Ship Propellor Company expressly for that purpose. No less than eight different screws were tried including four to the design of Francis Smith and three by Bennett Woodcroft. A summary of the results was afterwards published by Thomas Guppy in a paper presented to the Institution of Civil Engineers in 1845. This showed that the greatest speed was attained with a screw designed by Smith having a diameter of 5ft 9in and a pitch of 8ft. In the absence of theoretical data, those conducting the trials resorted to various improvisations and sections were cut from both the leading and trailing edges of screws covered by Woodcroft's patent. This resulted in less slip than had previously been experienced, and the speed attained was proportionally higher for a lower horsepower output than had been achieved by the most successful screw designed by Francis Smith. At this stage however, the trials were terminated as The Ship Propeller Company required the *Archimedes* for other service. A propeller of the amended Woodcroft design was afterwards tried out very successfully on the *Napoleon*, a vessel built by Augustin Normand of Le Havre but engined by John Barnes of Manchester.

The screw first chosen for the *Great Britain* was based on Smith's patent. It consisted of four separate iron forgings riveted together to form the central boss. Six arms, each 6in thick, were welded to the boss and blades shaped from $\frac{7}{8}$in iron plate were riveted to the extremities of the arms. The blades themselves were quite substantial, each measuring 2ft 7in at the narrowest point and 4ft 4$\frac{1}{2}$in on their circumference. The height of each blade was 2ft 9in. The overall diameter of the propeller was 15ft 6in and the pitch was 25ft. It weighed 3tons 17cwt. The problem of blade erosion due to the impingement of water at a high velocity on the leading edges of the blades was already appreciated, and attempts were made to minimise this by shaping and finishing these edges as accurately and as smoothly as possible. This was achieved by mounting the propeller on a faceplate and planing the surfaces with a suitable tool. Finally, according to Guppy, the propeller was given several coats of paint, rubbed smooth and varnished.

Compared with modern marine propellers, this six-bladed screw lacked the inherent strength of a single casting, an obvious source of weakness being the rivets which joined the blades to the central arms. The area presented to the water was small in relation to the diameter which led *The Times* correspondent to describe it on the day of the launch as a 'skeleton screw'. Nevertheless, it was the true

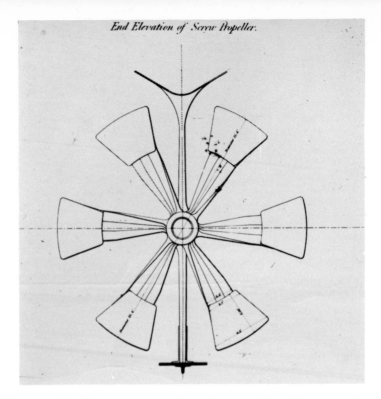

The original six-bladed screw and the pintle-type rudder. This screw suffered severe damage and was replaced during the winter refit of 1845–46

forerunner of the massive propellers weighing in excess of 50 tons which are cast today in complex copper-base alloys for giant super-tankers and passenger liners such as the QE2.

It is interesting to note that when a model of the *Great Britain* was recently tested in the Vickers Ship Model Experimental Tank at St Albans, it was shown that the propeller itself—a scaled-down version of the original screw—was remarkably efficient. The distance between the hull and the propeller was however judged to be too small, for it led to an undesirable interference with the flow and gave an overall propeller efficiency of about two-thirds of that considered normal for a modern screw.

It is apparent that Brunel, who was not given to self-doubt, considered the screw to be the most experimental feature of the *Great Britain* and his anxiety over the outcome can be discerned in a letter written to Guppy in August 1843 during the fitting out period. Commenting on the decision to adopt screw propulsion he wrote :

if all goes well we shall all gain credit but, *"quod scriptum est manet"*, if the result disappoint anybody, my written report

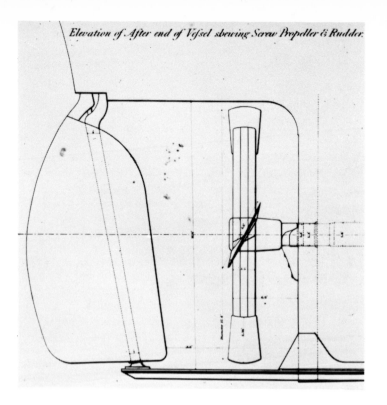

will be remembered by everybody, and I shall have to bear the storm.

The result of all my anxious thoughts—for I assure you I feel more anxious about this than most things I have had to do with—is first that we must adopt as a principle not to be departed from, that all mechanical difficulties of construction must in fact be lost sight of in determining the most perfect form—if we find that the screw determined upon cannot be made (but what cannot be done?), then it is quite time enough to try another form.

The problems relating to the design of the screw were of a relatively minor nature when compared with those that followed from its adoption. Although elimination of the paddleboxes would simplify construction, they had already begun to take shape which meant that much of the hull had to be re-designed. The major problem however concerned the engines. Brunel at first thought that he would be able to retain with certain modifications the engines that had been designed to drive the paddlewheels, but this was found to be impracticable. There was no alternative but to build another set of engines and this the company decided to do in their own recently completed engineworks. Humphys, seeing that his own trunk engine was rejected, resigned his position as engineer superintendent and the vacant post was offered, on Brunel's advice, to Thomas Guppy with responsibility for the construction of both the hull and the machinery.

Although nominally the relationship between Guppy and Brunel was that of director and principal adviser to the board, Guppy's reputation has always been overshadowed by Brunel's genius, and he has rarely been given the credit due to him for his major contribution in dealing with the day-to-day problems of building the largest ship in the world in a basic material of which there was barely twenty years' experience. He has been successively described as a merchant, an inventor and an engineer—a combination of talents not uncommon among the early Victorian entrepreneurs. Guppy was certainly a man of some wealth, for he is known to have invested nearly £15,000 of his own money in the GWSC. As an inventor he is credited with three patents awarded to him between 1824 and 1843. The first dealt with the provision of double pole masts for use in sloops and fore and aft rigged vessels, while the second had no nautical association being concerned with a technique for granulating sugar. His third patent, No 9779, granted to him on 15 June 1843 was obviously associated with his work on the *Great Britain* and contained a number of proposals relating to the construction of 'metal ships'.

Some were hardly practical, but at least two showed features which were probably adopted by Brunel. One related to the construction of false internal sides and bottoms of iron ships, and the other involved the fitting of airtight thwarts and seats to iron lifeboats. The four iron lifeboats which the *Great Britain* carried on her upper deck were designed by Guppy, and it is probable that these buoyancy provisions were incorporated. Less inspired were his suggestions to substitute copper plates for iron in vulnerable positions above and below the waterline, and his proposal to rivet a copper sheathing over an iron hull in the same way that timber ships were protected. Both these suggestions had the laudable aim of preventing fouling of a ship's bottom, but he was obviously not familiar with the problems of electrolytic corrosion already recognised by many shipbuilders, and which would have surely occurred had either of these ideas been adopted. This was one of the disadvantages of using iron, and eventually a number of proprietary chemical treatments were introduced specifically for this purpose.

Despite Guppy's energy and zeal, progress with the *Great Britain* was not fast. Work continued throughout the years 1841 and 1842 and gradually the vessel took shape in her final form. Brunel laid the same emphasis on longitudinal strength as he had done earlier with the *Great Western*. There is evidence to show that other ship-builders were beginning to realise the significance of this approach, but Brunel was the first to adopt this solution for the construction of a large iron ship. Iron lent itself readily to this form of fabrica-tion and iron girders were available with a range of profiles. Brunel selected ten large U-shaped girders or kelsons which were laid over the transverse ribs at the bottom of the ship. These were covered with an iron deck $\frac{3}{8}$in thick which was joined to the upper ends of the girders by means of separate angle iron sections, thus forming a cellular structure of great strength and rigidity. The kelsons were 3ft 3in deep and were fabricated from $\frac{1}{2}$in and $\frac{7}{16}$in plate; those in the centre extended throughout the length of the vessel while those on the sides terminated at the slope in the ship's bottom. The keel plate was $\frac{7}{8}$in thick; it consisted of a series of plates 20in wide which were fire welded into lengths of between 50 and 60ft. Each length was joined by means of scarfs 18in wide, and the joints were riveted over with the rivets positioned $4\frac{1}{2}$in apart. For extra strength the thickness of the keel plate was increased to 1in where contact might be made during grounding.

One of the most remarkable features was the fabrication of the stem which was welded to make one piece 18ft long. The ribs were formed principally of angle iron, 6in x $3\frac{1}{2}$in x $\frac{5}{8}$in, which was arranged at 18in centres in the midships section, but the interval was extended to 24in at the extremities where smaller ribs measur-ing 6in x $2\frac{1}{2}$in and 4in x 3in were used. Additional strength was given to the engineroom by riveting another angle section to each rib. There were nine of these double ribs and sixteen additional transverse ribs—a wise measure in view of the weight of the engines and boilers.

Several different thicknesses of plate were used for the ship's sides. Adjacent to the keel plate there were four rows $\frac{11}{16}$in thick, the area of the plates being 6ft to 6ft 6in long by 3ft wide. Then the thickness was reduced to $\frac{5}{8}$in up to the deep load water line, and in order to save top weight the plates above this level were gradually reduced to $\frac{3}{8}$in thick. The plates were scarfed and riveted along the entire length of the ship so that the vessel has always been described as 'clinker-built'. Most of the earlier iron ships were constructed with simple butt joints, probably with a single strap. Claxton reported that this type of joint had been tested in comparison with an overlapping scarf joint and the latter had been proved to be 20 per cent stronger.

Two bilge keels were fitted on either side of the centreline of the ship. Each was 110ft long and comprised two angle iron sections, 5in x 5in x 1in, riveted to the hull with a middle plate 1¼in thick. The under edges were level with the underside of the keel, so that when docking the ship, long baulks of timber could be placed across the dock supporting the weight of the vessel—particularly the engines and boilers—equidistant from the centreline. This was another indication of Brunel's foresight, when judged by the standards of the day, in dealing with problems arising from the massive size of the vessel.

In addition to the iron deck immediately above the longitudinal girders described on page 37, the ship had four other decks. These comprised an upper cargo deck, the main deck, a middle or promenade deck and finally the upper deck which was flush along the entire length of the ship. The cargo deck was made of iron plates ranging from $\frac{5}{16}$ to $\frac{9}{16}$ in thick, the remaining three decks being formed by heavy pine planks. In the case of the main deck the planks were 5in thick and were arranged athwartships to give transverse stiffness. When fully laden the main deck corresponded with the waterline, and Brunel considered that transverse rather than longitudinal stiffness was required at this point. The ends of the planks were firmly bolted through two longitudinal stringers of Baltic pine to the shelf plates which were 3ft wide by $\frac{5}{8}$in thick; the latter were securely fixed to the sides. The middle deck was similarly constructed except that the deck planks were 4in thick, and were placed lengthwise, as was the timber used for the upper deck— described as red pine. The side plates at the level were strengthened by an outside iron strap, 6in x 1in, and by additional straps measuring 7in x 1in which were welded in lengths of 60ft and riveted to the inner sides of the upper line of plates. Two massive ties of Baltic pine, each with a cross-sectional area of 340 sq in, were bolted to the ribs and the shelf plate at the upper deck level, and ran the entire length of the ship.

There were two fore and aft bulkheads and five transverse bulkheads which effectively divided the ship into six compartments. Three of the transverse bulkheads were extended as far as the upper deck. The first, which separated the forecastle from the forward passengers' cabins, was specially reinforced in case of collision. The second bulkhead was at the forward end of the combined boiler and engineroom, and the third formed the after end of the engineroom. A hole was cut in this bulkhead for the propeller shaft and a suitable collar was fitted to prevent any possible leakage from one compartment to another. There was also a watertight door to enable the engineroom staff to inspect the shaft in the stern passage. The remaining two bulkheads terminated at the promenade deck. One separated the after coal bunkers from the after cargo hold while the other was close to the stern of the ship.

Between bulkheads were the joists for supporting the decks which were formed from 3in angle iron with a joist bar measuring 5in x $\frac{1}{2}$in riveted on the side. The joists were spaced about 2$\frac{1}{2}$ft apart and the deck planks were fastened to the angle iron by screws from below. Finally, to prevent the hull from springing horizontally, diagonal tension bars were arranged between the decks and the side frames.

Altogether there were about 1040 tons of iron in the ship, principally in the form of iron plates and angle sections as described above. Joining was by fire welding or riveting—in many cases double riveting was employed. The standard of workmanship throughout was consistently high and although progress was slow there were no precedents for many of the constructional problems that were encountered. The sheer size and weight of many of the components must have presented difficulties especially since there was no tradition of iron ship building in Bristol, unlike in Liverpool or London.

The problems of 'materials handling' rarely worried early Victorian engineers when labour was plentiful and cheap, but although the company had no qualms about employing several hundred men on the construction of the *Great Britain,* they were determined that the number of seamen in her crew should be kept to a minimum. This meant that the sails had to be easy to handle and consequently, in order to obtain sufficient area of canvas, more than the usual number of masts were required. Originally it was intended to fit five masts, but this number was increased to six. These were described officially as fore, main, one, two, three and four but are reported to have been known familiarly by the days of the week from Monday to Saturday—a sensible amendment in view of the likelihood of confusion between 'fore' and 'four'. Only the main mast had yards and 'square' sails; the others were schooner rigged and officially the *Great Britain* was described as a six-masted schooner with standing bowsprit. Claxton afterwards reported that the sails could be handled by thirty men which was far less than on the ships of the line of the day. There were two other interesting developments embodied in the design of the rigging which show how Brunel sought to improve upon the techniques evolved through centuries of shipbuilding tradition. Firstly iron rigging in the form of stranded wire rope was adopted instead of hemp because it was thought to offer two-thirds less resistance than hemp when going into the wind. Secondly, with the exception of the main mast, all the masts were hinged at the upper deck level so that they could be

A model of the original engines in the Science Museum at South Kensington. Four single expansion engines were arranged in an inverted-vee form; each cylinder had a diameter of 88in

lowered if necessary—again to reduce resistance when under engine power alone. Neither of these innovations proved to be particularly successful and were to be altered during the first major refit, but they are further evidence of how an engineer with flair and an original mind could initiate new practices in shipbuilding which were eventually to be widely adopted.

Brunel used the same approach when designing the rudder and steering gear. He realised that the water thrust from the screw would make it more difficult to turn the rudder, and therefore decided to use a balanced rudder which was pivoted at about one-third of the distance from the forward edge. This type of rudder was afterwards the subject of some criticism but was generally adopted from the 1860s onwards. The steering gear for actuating the rudder was conventional with the wheel being positioned at the stern.

When the *Great Britain* was launched much of her machinery had not been installed. Work had however been in progress on the construction of her engines, boilers and the gear for stepping up the propeller shaft speed ever since the directors acted on Brunel's recommendations on screw propulsion. Considerable care was taken with the design of the boilers to ensure a sufficient supply of steam under all conditions of service. The solution adopted was to contruct three boilers within a single casing measuring 34ft long by 31ft wide with a height of 21ft 8in. There were two stokeholds fore and aft, and the boilers had four furnaces at each end making twelve in each stokehold. Each furnace had a separate course of flues which followed an 'S' shaped path and terminated in a common up-take. The total surface area of the grate bars was 360 sq ft and the total area of the furnace surface was 1248 sq ft. The flue gases were exhausted through a single funnel which had a diameter of 8ft. The funnel was given a slight rake of about 2 degrees, although it has been shown incorrectly by several artists to have been set vertical. In accordance with the practice of the day the boilers steamed on salt water which was pumped to an annular jacket around the base of the funnel. This served both as a feed heater and a gravity tank from which each boiler was fed. Provision was made to blow-down each boiler periodically to prevent excessive formation of brine, a number of small brine pipes being led to a common blow off pipe of 6in diameter located in each stokehold.

Various figures have been given for the boiler steam pressure ranging from 15 to 5 lb/sq in but since gravity feed was employed it is likely that the latter figure was nearer the mark. This was the steam pressure generated by the boilers of the *Great Western* and would have been in keeping with the practice of the day. Boiler explosions were still a common occurrence in the 1840s and marine boiler design generally lagged behind that of locomotive boilers. Steam was discharged from each boiler through what was described as a 'shut-off valve'. This appears to have been an ordinary screw down stop valve operated by a conventional handwheel. The shut-off valves were located at the after end of each boiler and they discharged into a common steam pipe with an outlet at each end. The diameter of each outlet was 2ft 4in. There were manholes for inspection at the top of each boiler and also spring-loaded safety valves. These were linked with a waste steam pipe which was located on the after side of the funnel.

It is apparent that the engines built to drive the screw owed little to Francis Humphys' original design. They were certainly not trunk engines in the accepted form, as a separate piston and connecting rods were fitted. The basic configuration comprised four cylinders,

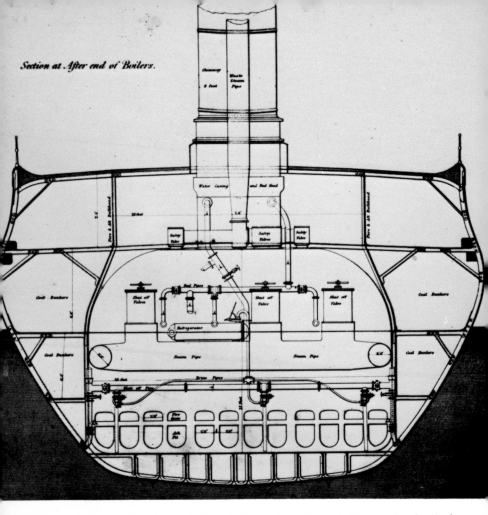

A view of the after end of the boilers looking forward. The two longitudinal bulkheads and the ten iron kelsons laid over the transverse ribs at the bottom of the ship can be clearly seen

each of 88in diameter, arranged in pairs low down in the ship and inclined at an angle of about 60 degrees, and it is interesting to note that a patent for inclined direct acting marine engines was taken out in 1822 by Marc Brunel. Guppy stated that originally the cylinders were to have an 80in diameter, but that they were increased in size in order to benefit from expansive working of the steam. Maudslay Sons and Field had submitted a design for the paddle engines providing for four cylinders of 75in diameter, and it is possible that the company used this as a basis for their own calculations. From a manufacturing point of view, four cylinders of 88in diameter were undoubtedly easier to cast and machine than two of 120in diameter which Brunel had called for in the earlier stages of the design. Steam was admitted to each cylinder through a throttle valve and a piston-type expansion valve of 20in diameter operated from eccentrics. The piston valve was adjustable so that steam could be shut off from the cylinder at a pre-determined point of the piston stroke. On trials, the most suitable position was found to be when the piston had travelled 1ft which was one sixth of its normal stroke. The steam inlet ports measured 2ft 6in by 8in and the steam was exhausted through outlet ports measuring 2ft 6in by 2ft 4in. The exhaust steam was led through an eduction pipe of 1ft 9in diameter to two wrought iron condensers set athwartships, each serving a pair of cylinders.

The covers of the main cylinders were large webbed castings fitted with spring loaded relief valves, certain of the webs being extended to form the crosshead guide. Each connecting rod was linked to the massive wrought iron overhead crankshaft or main shaft manu-factured by the Mersey Ironworks. Its weight—16 tons before machining—was supported by two huge A-frames which extended down to the bottom frames and were also connected to cross beams at deck level. The main shaft was 17ft long and its greatest diameter was 2ft 4in. The main bearing journals were 2ft diameter and each bearing cover was held in place by 3in diameter studs fitted with hexagon nuts and lock nuts. The cranks were 1ft 3in wide and the throw of the cranks was 3ft. A particularly interesting feature of its design was the provision of a 10in passage bored through the entire shaft for the circulation of cooling water. At the centre of the shaft was located a large drum with a diameter of 18ft 3in which carried the driving chains for the propeller shaft. At its extremities, in addition to the main connecting rods and eccentrics previously described, the crank pins were joined to the connecting rods of the hot well air pumps, one of which was fitted to each condenser. The engineroom auxiliary machinery was completed by a pair of hot water or boiler feed pumps and bilge pumps, each set being driven from a lever attached to an air pump crosshead. Since there was no point in recirculating the condensate, the air pump discharge was led overboard just below the waterline. Bilge pumps were fitted in each watertight compartment, their total capacity being 7000 gallons per min.

With the increasing size of marine steam engines certain refine-ments were introduced to assist engineers when carrying out routine inspections and overhauls. They mainly took the form of manholes or inspection covers and in the *Great Britain,* in addition to those fitted on top of the boilers, manholes were incorporated

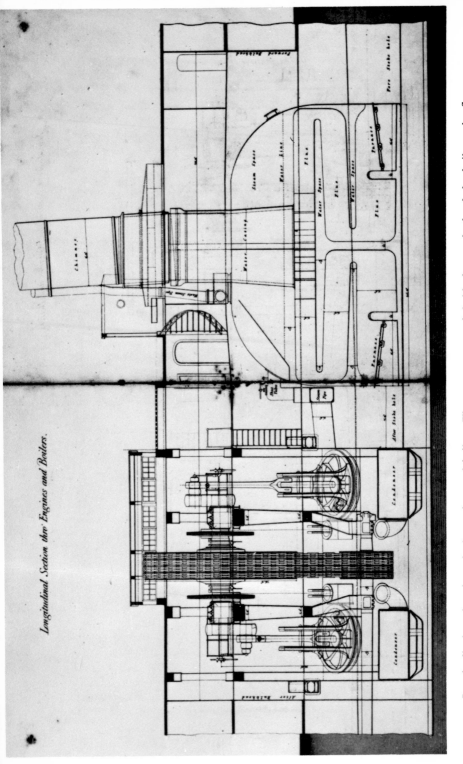

Longitudinal Section thro' Engines and Boilers.

Longitudinal section through the engines and boilers. There were two stokeholds fore and aft of the boilers; the flue gases were discharged through a single funnel which had a slight rake, a feat overlooked by many artists in their representation of into the engine cylinder covers and also in the pistons so that it was possible to examine the bottom of the cylinders without difficulty. This was a sensible arrangement since split pins and other foreign bodies always had a tendency to accumulate in such normally inaccessible places. The pistons were shaped in sections like a frustrum of a cone. Each had ten ribs and the sides were 10in deep; the piston rods were 9in diameter.

When in operation, the piston and connecting rods, the overhead shaft and the various other actuating rods must have been an impressive sight, but the dominating feature of the engineroom was the massive drum which drove the propeller shaft. This was so large that it extended above the upper deck into a specially constructed housing. The design maximum speed of the engines of the *Great Britain* was actually 18 rpm, and it was decided that at this speed, the propeller should rotate at 53 rpm. With the size of engines fitted, the use of a train of gearwheels making positive engagement would have been out of the question and Brunel had already criticised this system, employed on the *Archimedes*. He decided instead to adopt a system of chain drive with four pitched chains transmitting motion from the larger drum on the crankshaft to a smaller drum of 6ft diameter situated at the inboard end of the propeller shaft and in the same vertical plane as the main drum. It was necessary to limit the weight of the main drum as much as possible in view of its location above the waterline and it therefore took the form of a large spoked wheel with sixteen spokes linking the hub to the outer rim. Additional strength was given by an inner reinforcing ring and all parts were joined by riveting. Both drums were recessed to ensure that the chain links bedded in them securely without slipping; blocks of teak and lignum vitae were fitted on the drums and the interstices engaged the teeth on the insides of the chains. Brunel was aware that the links might stretch in service and great care was taken in their manufacture to minimise this risk. After forging each link was reheated to a dull red heat, then stretched $\frac{1}{8}$in and examined. After boring and planing, they were finished using the same gauge to ensure that each was identical before being case-hardened.

Conflicting reports were afterwards issued about the behaviour in service of this form of power transmission and it seems to have caused a certain amount of trouble, which is not surprising considering the chains together weighed 7 tons. In prinicple it was similar to the system patented by Joseph Maudslay, the third son of Henry Maudslay, in 1843. Maudslay used a six-grooved pulley fitted to the engine shaft which was linked with endless ropes to a smaller pulley keyed to the propeller shaft, an additional adjustable pulley

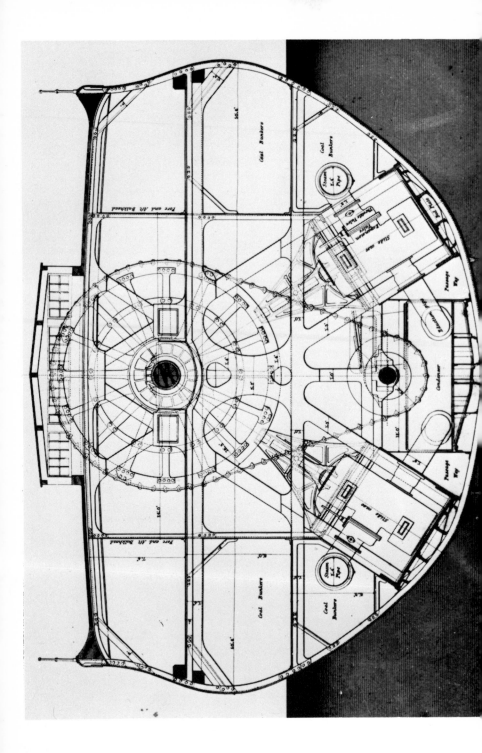

being provided to maintain tension on the ropes. Maudslay's system is supposed to have worked tolerably well but, in general, it can be said that all the methods adopted had limitations. No really satisfactory solution was found until the introduction of the compound engine, with its higher working speeds, made an increase in propeller shaft speeds unnecessary.

Another problem concerned the method of sealing the gland where the propeller shaft emerged from the hull. This was a constant source of trouble on all the early screwdriven vessels but was eliminated with John Penn's invention of the stern tube in 1855. On the *Great Britain* the packing used for this gland was reported to have been a combination of leather and copper, and it is perhaps significant that Brunel prudently placed a watertight bulkhead immediately forward of the shaft exit.

The propeller shaft itself was actually made in three sections. The inboard length, on which the lower drum was fixed, measured 28ft 3in in length, and had a diameter at the journals of 16in. It was supported at the forward end by bearings fitted in an extension of the same A-frames which held the crankshaft and main drum. The centre section was a remarkable example of plate fabrication since it was 61ft 8in long and was formed from two courses of plates, $\frac{3}{4}$in thick, that were riveted together with $1\frac{3}{4}$in countersunk rivets. The diameter of this hollow shaft was 30in. The outboard section or tail shaft was 25ft 6in long and the diameter at the journals was 17in. Brunel adopted the standard method of transmitting the thrust of the propeller to the ship's hull. This was somewhat crude but effective; a gunmetal plate, 2ft in diameter, was attached to the inboard end of the propeller shaft and this bore up against a steel plate of similar size which was fixed firmly to the engine frame and the hull of the ship. A stream of water was directed on to the plates at their point of contact.

The reference to the use of steel rather than iron for this highly stressed component is an interesting example of the restricted application of steel—then a comparatively expensive material—in the period immediately before cheap Bessemer steel became available. During the 1840s steel in Britain was still being made by the crucible process invented by Huntsman in the eighteenth century and the price was about five times that of iron.

It became apparent as work progressed that costs generally would have to be reviewed, and that the expenditure would greatly

Opposite: A section through the centre of the engineroom looking forward. Despite the size of the cylinders the dominating feature was the massive spoked wheel for the chain drive which was required to step up the speed of the propeller shaft

exceed the first estimate. On the day of the launch *The Times*
reported that instead of costing £76,000, as originally intended, the
vessel would probably cost £90–100,000. The nation-wide interest
in the vessel demonstrated by the vast gathering at the launch was
therefore particularly gratifying to the company whose only source
of income was that derived from the *Great Western*.

It was obviously essential to press forward with the installation
of the engines and boilers, and complete the fitting out as quickly
as possible, but costs continued to mount up until the overall total,
inclusive of the sum spent in setting up the shipyard and engine
works, was more than double the original estimate. Details are
given in an appendix. There were, however, other problems ahead
which the board of directors could not afford to ignore, since they
arose from the limitations of Bristol as a port and serious commercial competition from a Liverpool-based steamship company, then
operating under the rather ponderous title of British and North
American Royal Mail Steam Packet Company.

3 · Fitting Out and the Early Voyages

It can be argued that many of the difficulties which faced the GWSC in 1844 and the years immediately following had their origins in the eighteenth and early nineteenth centuries, when the struggle for commercial supremacy between Bristol and Liverpool began to be resolved in favour of the northern port. The geographical advantages of Liverpool were ultimately to prove decisive but undoubtedly the inertia of those responsible for the Bristol port facilities contributed to the city's partial decline.

Early in the eighteenth century, Bristol was becoming inadequate as a port, for ships were increasing in size. A floating dock was constructed at Sea Mills in 1712—the third to enter service in Great Britain—but its value was limited, and most large ships still had to anchor in the Bristol Channel at the mouth of the Avon and unload their cargoes into lighters. In 1765, John Smeaton was commissioned to report on the enlarging and modernising of the City Docks, but no action was taken until 1804, when William Jessop, a pupil of Seaton, began a radical reconstruction programme which took five years to complete. Although this resulted in the provision of a large wet dock, which extended into the heart of the city, it was still a case of 'too little and too late' since the facilities at Liverpool were by then far superior. Jessop's scheme was nevertheless ingenious. The Avon was diverted to a more southerly course through the New Cut and nearly two miles of its old bed were sealed off by locks to form the Floating Harbour. Water for this new dock was provided by the Frome and through a feeder canal cut through from the upper Avon. Unfortunately the rocky floor of the old river bed made dredging difficult and eventually restricted the size of the vessels using the Floating Harbour.

The company had selected a site on the south side of the Floating Harbour for their dry dock and works and, although the draught of the *Great Britain* in her unladen condition had not presented any problems on floating out, frustrating delays were caused and further expenses incurred when the time came to move the vessel through the two parts of locks which connected the 'Float' to the Avon and the sea.

An historic photograph of the *Great Britain* taken by Fox-Talbot, the pioneer photographer, in 1844 when the vessel was lying in the Floating Harbour. This is thought to be one of the first photographs ever taken of a ship

The first difficulty was encountered when the attempt was made in April 1844 to move the vessel out of the Wapping Dock for the second time after the engines and boilers had been installed. Although her increased weight caused her to draw considerably more water than on the day of the launch, the operation should have been effected smoothly. But for some unaccountable reason she refused to pass across the sill of the dock. Soundings were taken and the level of the water in the Float was raised by 18in on two separate days—but still she refused to budge. Eventually, early in May, a mathematical instrument maker of Bristol, J. M. Hyde, descended to the dock bottom in a diving apparatus of his own invention where he found that a large plank and other items of timber had become wedged under the ship's bottom. With the aid of a rope and chain these obstacles were removed, and the *Great Britain* once more moved into the Float and moored near the Clifton Gas Works. It was while she was in this position that Fox-Talbot, the pioneer photographer, visited Bristol and took the photograph shown on page 50. This is probably another celebrated 'first' to the credit of the *Great Britain* since it is thought to be the first photograph ever taken of a ship, though the directors are unlikely to have appreciated the significance of this fact.

They had now reached an apparent impasse in their negotiations with the Bristol Dock Company concerning the widening of the locks at the entrance to the Float. It seems hardly credible that the company had not secured a firm undertaking that the locks would be widened before proceeding to build their mammoth vessel with a beam 5½ft greater than the opening of the existing locks. It would appear, to use a modern phrase, that a 'disastrous failure in communications' had occurred. Both Guppy and Claxton in subsequent published accounts have shown that there was probably a culpable lack of foresight on the part of the board and Claxton admitted that it had been their original intention to tow the vessel out light and sail her elsewhere to fit the engines. Since this plan had been abandoned in 1839, five years previously, there had been no lack of time to press for the necessary alterations to be put in hand. Brunel himself, in his capacity of chief engineer to the Dock Company, had carried out improvements in 1833, and in a later report recommended that the locks should be widened from 45ft to 54ft.

In April 1844 the *Bristol Mirror* reported that, because of the deadlock, the correspondence between the two companies had been sent to the Board of Trade for their adjudication. The Board decided in favour of the Dock Company who were bound by an Act of Parliament to keep the facilities of the port open to all shipping. The question of the indemnity to be paid to the Dock Company remained an obstacle to a settlement and in the opinion of the paper it was unlikely that sea trials would take place before the autumn. Their correspondent showed a wry sense of humour when he likened the *Great Britain* to 'a fattened weasel in a farmer's granary growing too big for the hole through which it got in'. Another comment, no doubt inspired by the penal system of the day but in a more optimistic vein, referred to 'the great prisoner at the bar who cannot remain in dock forever but will doubtless soon be transported beyond the seas'.

One of the more fortunate consequences of this enforced delay was that the fitting out could be completed without undue haste. The same high standard of craftsmanship was maintained in the construction and furnishing of the cabins and saloons. On the middle or promenade deck immediately below the upper deck, two large promenade saloons were situated. The forward or second class saloon measured 67ft by 21ft 9in and the after or first class saloon was 110ft 6in long by 22ft wide. The saloons were positioned on the centreline and were surrounded by gangways and cabins. They were lit with oil lamps and well ventilated through overhead skylights which opened out onto the upper deck. The dining saloons were situated on the main deck below. The Grand Saloon for the

Plan view of a model in the Science Museum, South Kensington. This model was presented to the Museum by Thomas Guppy, a director and the superintending engineer of the Great Western Steamship Company

first class passengers was certainly the largest single compartment in any passenger vessel afloat and measured 93ft 6in by 30ft. The second class saloon was 61ft long with a width of 21ft 9in. Again cabins were arranged on each side making a total of 26 single and 113 double cabins on both decks. The height of saloons and cabins on both decks was 8ft 3in so that there was a feeling of spaciousness not always experienced on modern passenger vessels.

The fourth deck, known as the upper cargo deck, had a stowage capacity for about 1000 tons of general cargo, and beneath this deck in the forward and after parts of the ship were situated iron fresh water tanks. The officers and seamen were quartered in the fo'c'sle, but the engineroom staff lived amidships adjacent to the machinery compartments. One of the warmest places in the ship must have been the galley which was immediately above the boilers and close to the base of the funnel.

The lifeboats designed by Guppy were installed during the fitting out stage. They comprised four large iron boats located in davits—

A recent model of the *Great Britain* in the Bristol Museum shows the vessel as originally completed in 1844

two on each side of the ship—and a further boat which was positioned amidships on the upper deck. The lifeboats could carry four hundred people, which meant that there was ample room for a full complement of passengers and the crew.

Other additional apparatus fitted at this time included an electrically-operated log patented by Edward Massey. Massey was granted three patents, in 1834, 1836 and finally No 10210 on 1 June 1844, and his log was certainly one of the earliest examples of the use of electricity at sea. The apparatus described in his third patent consisted of a small rotor or impeller which was towed through the water behind the ship. On the ship's side the rotating cable was connected through a rack and pinion to a small brass plate. When the rotor had made a certain number of revolutions the brass plate was moved to join the ends of two copper wires which were part of an electrical circuit containing a battery and a register or dial. The battery was usually located on the upper deck and the register could be fixed in any convenient position, such as the captain's cabin. It contained three pointers, one revolution of each showed that the ship had travelled one, ten and a hundred nautical miles

A close-up of the bow of the model in the Science Museum. The Royal Arms of Great Britain and other details were picked out in gold leaf on the ship as shown here

respectively; and by observing the number of graduated units travelled by the pointer of the first index in one minute, it was possible to ascertain the ship's speed in knots.

This instrument was to become a useful aid to navigation but remained secondary in importance to the mariners' compass. At least two compasses are known to have been fitted on the *Great Britain*—a precaution which was thought necessary in some quarters because of her massive iron hull. The effect of a large mass of iron on the compass performance was quoted during the 1830s as a major disadvantage of iron ships, for despite a thorough series of investigations by the Admiralty and various independent authorities, there were still many who doubted the reliability of a compass used under these conditions. In 1835 a certain Captain Johnson, working under the direction of the Admiralty, had carried out some experiments aboard the *Garry Owen* to ascertain the most suitable position for a compass in an iron ship. Johnson's work was a prelude to a more thorough investigation undertaken by Professor Airy, the Astronomer Royal in 1838-9, who used the vessel *Ironside* built by John Grantham for his observations.

Airy subsequently published his findings in the *United Services Journal*. His recommendations for compass correction proved so successful that they soon became generally adopted, and the advocates of iron were able to claim, several years before the *Great Britain* was completed, that after compasses in iron ships had been corrected they were generally more accurate than those fitted in timber ships, where there was often some risk of deflection due to iron bolts and other iron objects in the immediate vicinity of the compass. Airy nevertheless recognised that compasses on iron ships had to be checked regularly, especially after a vessel had been in dock for a long period, and there is evidence that this routine was carried out on board the *Great Britain*.

Problems with the compass were probably far from the minds of the directors of the company during the summer of 1844, as they watched the months gradually slip past, and as another summer season of lucrative passenger and cargo traffic was denied to the largest and most powerful ship in the world. When the keel plates of the *Great Britain* had been laid down in 1839, the fortunes of the company had been riding high, especially as their early competitors from Liverpool and elsewhere were beginning to experience difficulties. The Transatlantic Shipping Company was wound up in July 1840, and the British and American Steam Navigation Company never recovered from the loss of the *President* in March 1841.

The challenge from Liverpool was soon taken up however by the British and North American Royal Mail Steam Packet Company, formed in 1840 by Samuel Cunard, a native of Nova Scotia. Cunard had previously been engaged in the shipping business in Canada. He was a man of great ability and drive, and in fact possessed many of the same characteristics as Brunel. His plan for a successful transatlantic steamship service was simple. The company should operate at least three ships, a regular service should be maintained throughout the year and the safety of the passengers should override all other considerations. In point of fact, Cunard was persuaded by Robert Napier to build four ships rather than three, and orders were placed with various shipbuilders on the Clyde. The first Cunarders—the *Britannia, Acadia, Caledonia* and *Columbia*—were modest ships compared with the *Great Britain*. They were built of timber and were paddle-driven; their engines, which were the conventional side-lever type, were about the same size as those fitted in the *Great Western*. In short they were designed within the limits of the technology of the day and as a result they were built quickly, at a moderate cost and in service soon gained a reputation for reliability. The Cunard Steamship Company, as it eventually came to be known, quickly became a formidable competitor to the Bristol-based company whose only source of income was that derived from the operations of the *Great Western*. In 1841 GWSC receipts fell by 50 per cent and despite fare reductions to attract more passengers this trend continued. In 1840 the cost of a single berth to New York had been 45gns. This was reduced in 1841 to 36gns and again in 1843 to 31gns. The number of vacant berths on each voyage however remained depressingly large with the cream of the traffic going to the Cunarders who operated on a slightly shorter sea-route from Liverpool to Boston via Halifax. *The Times* of 15 August 1842 reported that the *Columbia* had just completed an outward passage to Boston in 12 days 10 hours including a five hours stay at Halifax while the *Great Western* had taken over a day longer on a journey from Bristol to New York.

It is unlikely however that even the Cunard Company could have operated profitably on the passenger receipts alone, but they possessed one vital advantage over their competitors, namely a regular subsidy from the British Post Office in the form of a mail contract. This had been obtained by Samuel Cunard in 1838, nearly 18 months before his first vessel, the *Britannia,* was ready for service. The Admiralty had advertised for tenders to carry mails to Halifax, Nova Scotia, twelve times a year. Until then, all the steamships operating across the Atlantic had carried mail on a single voyage contract but it was decided to grant one company a monopoly at a reduced rate. The GWSC put in a tender for £45,000 for twelve voyages but Cunard offered to carry the mails on thirty voyages for £60,000. Much to the dismay of the Bristol-based company, Cunard's offer was accepted at once and there was much bitterness when they were not permitted to tender again on the same basis. Credit for obtaining this vital contract for Cunard has been given to James Melvill, a director of the company who, was also at that time Chief Secretary of the all-powerful East India Company, and was not without friends in high places. The directors of the GWSC managed to secure a House of Commons Enquiry through the political influence of the parent GWR, but were unable to reverse the decision. In 1842, they made a direct appeal to Sir Robert Peel, who was then Chancellor of the Exchequer, to be granted a mail contract between England and New York at the same rate that the Cunard Company were receiving for the Liverpool-Nova Scotia service. The appeal was signed by Kingston and Bright, the Chairman and Vice-Chairman, and Captain Claxton as Managing Director. It was written in extremely persuasive terms, and cited the company's pioneering role on the Atlantic steamship routes as well as services rendered by carrying despatches in the *Great Western* during the border disturbances which had recently occurred in Canada. The Chancellor was not impressed however, and no action was taken. The GWSC and the other shipping companies had to be content with the crumbs. They still continued to carry packets of mail on a private basis, the rates depending on the length of the packet. Examples of prices charged by the *Great Western* in 1843 were 6in long, 7s; 9in long, 11s; 12in long, 16s. The true value of the mail contract was to be revealed in 1846 when Samuel Cunard testified before a Select Committee of the House of Commons that his company over six years had received £3,295 per round voyage. This was equivalent to the fares of about fifty extra passengers in each direction and meant the difference between a respectable profit and a disappointing loss. There were however certain disadvantages relating to the mail contract. The ships had to carry a naval officer on board, and they could be commandeered as troopships in time of war. The Admiralty laid down certain conditions regarding their construction, and as late as 1850 were adamant against the use of iron for hull construction.

One lesson therefore that was learnt between the years 1837 and 1844 was that it was impossible to operate a service profitably with vessels of only a thousand tons burden without some form of subsidy. To those denied this assistance the only solution was to build larger ships with greater cargo-carrying capacities and Brunel's 'big ship' policy was fundamentally sound. In the late summer of 1844 it still appeared that it would never be put to the test and even

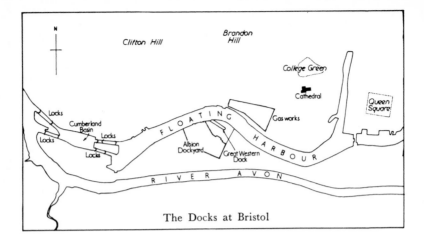

The Docks at Bristol

when agreement was finally reached with the Dock Company, there remained the task of moving the *Great Britain* through the two sets of locks into the Avon. By this time the building committee had the benefit of the experience of the newly appointed master, Captain James Hosken, who had held command of the *Great Western* from 1837 to 1843. Hosken was then 46 years old, and was undoubtedly the most experienced ocean-going steamship captain in the world. He had successfully completed sixty-four passages across the Atlantic —a feat which had been recognised by the underwriters at Lloyds who presented him with a gold watch when he left the *Great Western* in November 1843. He was born into a naval family; his father had been a warrant officer in the Royal Navy and he himself joined the service as a midshipman in 1810. Promotion had been slow when the Napoleonic wars ended. He was promoted Lieutenant in 1828 and went on half pay to assume command of a merchant ship trading between Liverpool and South America in 1833. His big opportunity came when he was offered the command of the *Great Western;* he still retained his substantiative rank of lieutenant and was not promoted to commander until 1853.

Like all concerned with the fortunes of the *Great Britain* the enforced inactivity when the ship was still imprisoned in the Float must have been particularly frustrating to Hosken. The vessel was finally moved through the inner set of locks into the Cumberland Basin on the night of 25 October. One source relates that a wooden cradle was sunk beneath her to give extra buoyancy and lift her clear of any obstruction. It was reported elsewhere that the lock was also widened for the occasion and then restored to its original form a few days afterwards. She remained in the Basin for a further six weeks; engine trials were carried out successfully, and she was lightened by removing stores and equipment where possible to permit her to pass through the outer locks into the Avon on the next high tide. This proved to be another difficult task. The appointed day was 11 December, and the operation began under the light of flares at 6.30 am when it was very dark and cold. Despite this early hour, thousands of people thronged every part of the Basin and Rownham Wharf waiting to see the *Great Britain* pass through the locks. Part of the stonework as well as the swing bridge had already been removed and at 7 am the vessel began to proceed towards the entrance of the lock. She was towed from her stern by two steam tugs with a third kept in reserve behind. At 7.15 am she entered the lock; it was then very nearly high tide but owing to the strong east wind the tide was 2ft below normal. When almost through she touched at the sides and Claxton, who was on board one of the tugs, ordered that she should be towed back into the basin. The tide had already started to fall and the decision was taken not a moment too soon.

During the remainder of the day work was carried out at a frantic pace under Brunel's supervision to make the lock still wider. A further attempt to tow her through was made in the evening and this time it was successful; the *Great Britain* finally emerged from her 'captivity' in the Float and was never to return during her active career. She was grounded that night prior to moving down the Avon on the morning tide. Brunel, who had an appointment in Wales, wrote to excuse himself for failing to keep the engagement. It was obviously an anxious time for him, since he wrote that he could not leave the ship until he saw her afloat again and clear of all her difficulties. In point of fact, the crisis was past and the rest of the operation proceeded smoothly. She was re-floated on the morning tide and at 8.5 am on 12 December began her journey down to the mouth of the river. She was towed by three tugs—two called *Sampson* and one named *Lion*. It was a triumphant procession; she moved gracefully through the water and was cheered by crowds of spectators who lined the banks of the river all the way.

The directors who were on board with their guests must have at last felt that they were about to gain some recompense for the tremendous outlay for the vessel—a sum which had just been further increased by £1330 4s 9d for the work carried out in widening the locks. They were determined that there should be no further delays, and sea trials began the very next day. Steam was raised during the forenoon and the ship got under way from the anchorage at Kingroad at 11.30 am. Brunel and Guppy instructed the chief engineer, H. S. Harman, to set the engine revolutions initially at 6 rpm which gave a speed of 4 knots. On passing Portishead at noon the speed of the engines was increased to $9\frac{3}{4}$ rpm and then to $10\frac{1}{2}$ rpm giving a ship's speed of 7 knots. The throttle valves remained open at that point for some time and then speed was increased once again to 12 rpm or 8 knots. Turning trials were then carried out near the Holms. With the helm hard down the ship came about in 9 minutes making a circle of rather more than half a mile diameter. Afterwards with the helm at 30 degrees she came round in 6 minutes and in less distance. Her steering capabilities were obviously satisfactory especially as it was recorded that only one man was required at the wheel.

While at the Holms, a dinner for seventy people was held in the saloon with Captain Hosken presiding. On the return run, the engines were operated closer to their designed maximum power. The speed was first increased to 13 rpm to give $8\frac{1}{4}$ knots and then to $16\frac{1}{2}$ rpm which was equivalent to 11 knots. As this was attained against a strong head wind and six of the twenty-four furnaces were not even lit, Brunel and Guppy had reason to be satisfied with the performance of the machinery. The vessel was drawing only $14\frac{1}{2}$ft at the stern, which meant that the propeller was not fully immersed, and that some loss of power was inevitable. However, they swept past the *Sampson,* the fastest paddleboat in the port and anchored once more at Kingroad at 6 pm to cheers from the vessels lying in the roadstead. It had been an auspicious beginning. During the trial the performance of the compass was watched carefully. It had previously been compensated, probably according to the methods recommended by Professor Airy, and it was recorded that the local attraction was less than aboard ships of timber construction.

Two further trials were held from Kingroad. The first took place on 8 January 1845 with 140 guests on board. These included many eminent engineers of the day such as George Rennie, Samuda a protagonist of the atmospheric railway, and the two principal British advocates of screw propulsion, Francis Smith and Bennett Woodcroft. The vessel was delayed nearly $4\frac{1}{2}$ hours because of fog, and Guppy afterwards said that the pilot was reluctant to move out of sight of land. Eventually another trip was made to the Holms and back. This was as successful as before, the engines eventually being worked up to 18 rpm on the homeward run which gave a speed of $11\frac{3}{4}$ knots. Turning manoeuvres were again performed off the Holms—a turn of 32 points was made in under 7 minutes and one of 16 points in 3 minutes 58 seconds.

On 20 January, a longer trial was held almost as far as Ilfracombe and back—a distance of about 100 miles being covered in 8 hours 34 minutes at average of over 11 knots. This promised well for the 'shakedown' voyage to London. The ship weighed anchor at 7 pm on Thursday 23 January; there was a minor mishap when the anchor fouled the wreck of a small schooner, the *Nova Creina*, which had sunk six weeks previously. Portions of her rigging were brought up, but the delay was not prolonged and by 9.40 pm the ship was once more abreast of the Holms with the engines making 14 rpm. The trip round Lands End and up the Channel was made in the teeth of gale force winds and was to be a severe test of the *Great Britain* and her crew. During the first watch on the 23rd speed was reduced so that adjustments could be made to the main bearings. The strong breeze increased to a gale during the night with frequent heavy squalls. This continued all the way round Lands End, and for a period the ship was making a little more than $5\frac{1}{2}$ knots. According to *The Times* correspondent who was on board for the trip, she rolled considerably, but this was only to be expected since she was so lightly laden. At 3.20 pm on Friday the 24th, a tremendous sea struck the starboard bow and almost brought her to a standstill. The huge wave drove in three 7in port lights or bullseyes, and damaged the upperworks carrying away a portion of the carved woodwork at the bow. After this the wind began to moderate and the jib, square mainsail and mizzen spencer were set as the *Great Britain* proceeded up-Channel. The weather remained favourable during 25 January. A brief stop was made during the afternoon off Cowes to land despatches, and at Spithead HMS *Apollo* cheered ship as the *Great Britain* passed close by.

The smoothest part of the passage was between Beachy Head and Dungeness when, with a stern sea, a speed of over 13 knots was attained. She anchored overnight in the Downs and next morning, when she got under way, there were about a hundred vessels watching her progress. This was in contrast to the earlier part of the voyage when practically every other ship had run for shelter. As she rounded the North Foreland, the wind again reached gale force and continued to blow hard WNW all the way up the Thames estuary. She was cheered by the *Prince Albert,* an American ship carrying emigrants to New York and by the passengers and crews of numerous river craft. Gravesend Reach was packed with ships, and another incident occurred in the shape of a minor collision with a collier brig which was said afterwards to be dragging her anchor. The bowsprit of the collier was carried away but no damage to the *Great Britain* was reported. She finally reached Woolwich at 3.30 pm on Sunday afternoon and moored at Blackwall.

The voyage had lasted $59\frac{1}{2}$ hours and had been accomplished at an average speed of $9\frac{1}{2}$ knots, which was commendable in the heavy seas encountered. There was no doubt that the screw propeller had performed well, although Guppy afterwards stated that he thought it was too small for the duty entrusted to it. Although the ship was light, the screw was never more than half out of the water even when the storm had been at its worst and, apart from an occasional slight acceleration of about half a revolution, it had never caused any fluctuation in the uniform rate of the engines. Hosken also endorsed Guppy's opinion about the behaviour of the screw. Unlike the members of building committee he had very little previous experience of screw propulsion, although his service on the *Great Western* had fully acquainted him with the deficiencies of paddle boxes. At the Institution of Civil Engineers on 4 March 1845 he predicted that the propeller would supersede paddles for seagoing vessels—a statement which probably raised the eyebrows of the more conservative members.

This was the occasion when Guppy presented a paper to a meeting of the Institution held under the chairmanship of the President, Sir John Rennie. The paper, which described in detail the construction of the *Great Britain*, was read to a distinguished audience containing many of the leading engineers of the day. The discussion which followed covered almost every aspect of the ship's performance and Guppy, Hosken, and Francis Smith who was also present, were closely questioned about her steering capabilities, the behaviour of the engines and gearing, and above all the screw. An interesting and prophetic comment came from Robert Stephenson who noted the similarity of the chains used for driving the propeller shaft with those used in the early locomotives which had since been discarded. The drum and chain drive had apparently performed well according to Guppy, but it was too early to forecast whether excessive wear or lengthening of the links would occur. The last speaker was Joshua Field, who mentioned the use of watertight bulkheads in a group of timber vessels constructed by Sir Samuel Bentham for the Admiralty, half a century earlier. Bentham's vessels had been noted for their extraordinary strength and efficiency, and Field complimented Guppy, and by inference Brunel on the mode of construction adopted.

Guppy's paper to the Institution was summarised in *The Times* on 6 March. The 'Thunderer' showed an almost proprietary interest in the ship, and every triumph and setback in her career were faithfully recorded for the benefit of the paper's readers. The steamship company made every effort to secure the maximum commercial advantage from the tremendous interest shown in their vessel. The public were allowed on board for the sum of 3s 6d a head; crowds thronged to Blackwall, and hawkers did a roaring trade selling prints of the ship for a 1d each on the quayside. Not all the visitors came away with favourable impressions, and many who were accustomed to the broader beam paddle vessels, thought she was too narrow for her length. One critic declared that her dark bulk and six bare poles monopolised the pool, but conceded that her 'iron bound strength inspired confidence'—a statement no doubt echoed by many of her passengers in the voyages that would follow.

Guppy's literary activities did not end with his paper since he agreed to collaborate with an enterprising publisher, one John Weale of Holborn, to produce a series of drawings with descriptive text showing all the important features of the vessel. It was intended to publish the work in four parts from 1 March 1845 at two-monthly intervals. Each part would cost 10s, and would be self-contained with drawings and text. A number of drawings were completed by an artist employed by Weale and Guppy corrected the proofs, but despite persistent pleas from Weale he never prepared the descriptive text. Eventually, after two years Weale published twenty-five drawings in a single volume for £1 5s. od. A number of copies of this work have survived and provide a permanent record of many of the more remarkable features of the vessel—it can only be regretted that the drawings are not accompanied by the comments of the man who—apart from Brunel—was responsible, more than any other, for her construction.

The *Great Britain* was to remain on the Thames until the early part of June, but the highlight of her stay was the visit of Queen Victoria on 22 April. The company took every care to make the Royal visit a memorable occasion. The ship was dressed overall, her decks were holystoned and carpets were specially laid in the saloons and on the gangways leading to the saloons and the engine-room. The band of the 1st Life Guards was engaged to play during the afternoon and the directors and other leading personalities, Brunel included, were on board to greet their distinguished guests.

The Queen accompanied by Prince Albert left Buckingham Palace at 2.30 pm and proceeded to Greenwich in an open carriage escorted by a detachment of Dragoons. At Greenwich she embarked in the Royal Yacht—the *Fairy*—which was driven by screw propulsion and had attained a speed of about 13 knots on trials. The short journey down river was however made at a more leisurely pace, since the Royal Yacht was preceded by the Lord Mayor of London who was present in his barge in his capacity of Conservator of the Thames. A number of river steamers followed the procession and a small armada of lesser craft were waiting at Blackwall—many of them dressed with flags for the occasion. Her Majesty was received by the chairman as she stepped on board but it was Hosken who conducted the party over the ship. The Queen expressed her

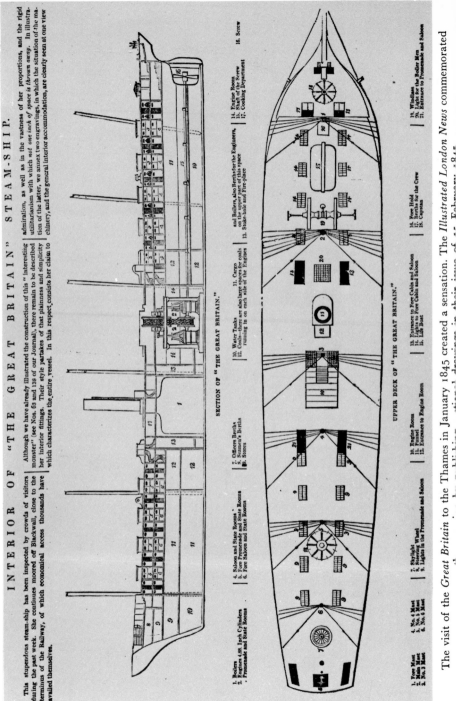

INTERIOR OF "THE GREAT BRITAIN" STEAM-SHIP.

This stupendous steam-ship has been inspected by crowds of visitors during the past week. She continues moored off Blackwall, close to the terminus of the Railway, of which economical access thousands have availed themselves.

Although we have already illustrated the construction of this "interesting monster" (see Nos. 63 and 138 of our Journal), there remain to be described her interior fittings. Their style partakes of that plainness and simplicity which characterize the entire vessel. In this respect, consists her claim to

admiration, as well as in the vastness of her proportions, and the rigid utilitarianism with which *not one inch of space is thrown away*. In illustration of the latter, we annex two engravings, in which the situation of the machinery, and the general interior accommodation, are clearly seen at one view

SECTION OF "THE GREAT BRITAIN."

1. Boilers	7. Officers Berths	and Boilers, also Berths for the Engineers,
2. Section of 88 Inch Cylinders	8. Seamen's Berths	on the upper part of this space
3. Promenade and State Rooms	9. Stores	13. Stoke-hole and Fire-place
4. Saloon and State Rooms	10. Water Tanks	14. Engine Room
5. Promenade and State Rooms	11. Coals—these are also large and cools	15. Shaft of the Screw
6. Fore Saloon and State Rooms	12. Cargo running in on each side of the Engines	16. Screw
		17. Cooling Department

UPPER DECK OF "THE GREAT BRITAIN."

1. Fore Mast	7. Skylight	13. Entrance to Fore Cabin and Saloon
2. Main Mast	8. Steering Wheel	14. Funnel
3. No. 3 Mast	9. Lights in the Promenade and Saloon	15. Entrance to Engine Room
4. No. 4 Mast	10. Engine Room	16. Fore Hold
5. No. 5 Mast	11. Funnel	17. Berths for the Crew
6. No. 6 Mast	12. Entrance to Engine Room	18. Capstan
	13. Entrance to Fore Cabin and Saloon	19. Windlass
	14. Lights to Fore Cabin and Saloon	20. Light for the Boiler Men
	15. Life Boat	21. Entrance to Promenade and Saloon

The visit of the *Great Britain* to the Thames in January 1845 created a sensation. The *Illustrated London News* commemorated amazement on being informed that the vessel was a third longer than the largest ship of the line in the Navy. She walked the whole length of the upper deck viewing the vessel from both the fo'c's'le and the stern. She then visited the saloons and state rooms where a model of the midships section of the ship and a working model of the engines and screw were shown to her. Brunel explained the features of the engines and the way in which the screw propelled the ship. Guppy then took the visitors to view the engineroom before they were conducted to the main dining-room where they were show models of three propellers—one representing the 6-bladed propeller fitted while another was of the 4-bladed screw held on board as a reserve. At this point Francis Smith presented the Queen with a gold model of the screw of the *Fairy* and Captain Claxton gave Her Majesty two copies of a pamphlet describing the *Great Britain*.

Royal patronage stimulated still further public interest in the vessel, which continued to be a centre of attraction as spring changed into summer. The directors were anxious to make two or three quick voyages as soon as possible to convince the travelling public of the safety of the vessel. Hosken had admitted this to the Prince Consort when he was questioned about the date of the maiden voyage. It had long been decided that she would operate from Liverpool where she could berth at any state of the tide. The booming cotton industry of Lancashire and good communications by rail, river and canal with other regions of the industrial North and Midlands had already made Liverpool a vast entrepôt where cargoes could more easily be obtained. Furthermore, the port dues were half those at Bristol and a continuous building programme promised to keep pace with the increasing demand for the port's facilities.

The decision was a wise one even if it meant severing all ties with the westcountry port. The steamship company had agents in Liverpool, Messrs Gibbs, Bright and Co who were linked with the GWSC through Robert Bright, one of the original directors. Many of the arrangements for the maiden voyage became the responsibility of the Liverpool agents who were busily employed during the early summer. The *Great Britain* at last left the Port of London, but instead of steaming direct to the Mersey called first at Plymouth and then Dublin. She attracted great crowds at Plymouth during her stay from 14 to 20 June; more than fifteen thousand people visited her at Millbay Pier which had just been completed for a cost of £30,000. On the last day she took five hundred at 5s a head for a trip round Eddystone lighthouse. The bearings ran hot again on the return journey and she was forced to stop, finally making Plymouth at reduced speed. The trouble could not have been very

The promenade deck. Her interior fittings were described by contemporary writers as being plain and simple—as indeed they were according to the standards of the age

serious as she left later that day for Dublin, calling at Falmouth briefly en route. So great was the public interest in the vessel, that the directors of the Dublin and Kingston Railway had paid the sum of £500 to induce the *Great Britain* to call at Dublin. It is not known whether this enterprising proposal brought a profit to the railway company but no doubt the GWSC was glad of the bonus. The *Great Britain* finally arrived at the Mersey at 10 pm on 3 July where there was another rousing welcome awaiting her, the estuary echoing with cheers and counter cheers from the *Great Britain* and the other ships in the port.

She was taken into the Queen's Graving Dock for a final examination and then towed out to prepare for her maiden voyage to New York which was scheduled for later that month. This was nearly delayed by the non-appearance of a sailing collier which was becalmed on passage from South Wales. One of the few disadvantages of Liverpool as a port was that it was some distance away from a good supply of steam coal. The early steamship operators had soon discovered the advantages of using coal from South Wales; Claxton reported that the *Great Western* consumed only 23 tons of Welsh steam coal a day as opposed to between 35 and 40 tons when the coal came from Lancashire, Scotland or Picton, Nova Scotia. The situation was saved by magnaminity of the Cunard Steamship Company who allowed the *Great Britain* to top up her bunkers from their coal depot at Liverpool.

Cunard could perhaps afford to be generous as they now had five ships on the Atlantic run which, until the arrival of the *Great Britain,* constituted a virtual monopoly as far as steamship services were concerned. The American-owned sailing packets still operated regularly between Liverpool and New York but they were mostly concerned with the emigrant traffic where the fares and the profit margins were low. GWSC made an attempt to attract passengers who wanted better facilities than those prevailing on the regular emi-

The *Great Britain* leaving Blackwall after her visit to the Thames during the early part of 1845 which lasted nearly five months

grant ships but preferred not to pay the single rate charge which had hitherto been in force on the Cunard ships and on the *Great Western*. They were able to do this because of the size of the *Great Britain* which had permitted the provision of forward and after dining-rooms and saloons as described on page 52. This enabled the Company to charge five rates ranging from 20 to 35 gns in contrast with the previous single fare of 30 gns.

It is not known how many people found these fares sufficiently attractive to participate in the maiden voyage because the newspapers of the day either omitted the figures or gave conflicting totals ranging between forty-five and sixty. It has been recorded that she carried 600 tons of cargo which, although not her total capacity, was a respectable beginning. The long awaited moment came shortly after 3 o'clock on the afternoon of Saturday 26 July, when she left her moorings in the Mersey accompanied by nine steamers with their decks packed with spectators. She proceeded slowly down river passing pier after pier which were also thronged with cheering crowds. A party of distinguished guests was on board including Admiral Sir Byam Martin RN and other prominent citizens from

At sea under steam and sail. Her early voyages across the Atlantic were marked with minor mishaps and her average crossing time was longer than that of most of the paddle steamers on the same route

Liverpool and the adjoining districts. The escorting steamers followed through the Rock Channel to the open sea as far as the north-east lightship. There they turned about while the guests aboard the *Great Britain* were taken off in the *Dreadnought*, a steam tug lent to the company for the occasion. Thereafter Brunel's 'great iron ship' steamed on alone to an almost audible sigh of relief from the shareholders of the steamship company. *The Times* commenting on her departure said 'the *Great Britain* is at length fairly launched forth upon her course upon the ocean', and no doubt the Bristol merchants murmured 'not a moment too soon.'

The maiden voyage took 14 days 21 hours, a time which was perhaps a little disappointing as the smaller Cunarders and the *Great Western* frequently beat this with a day or more in hand. The weather was not favourable, however, with strong westerly winds blowing during the greater part of the crossing. Her arrival in New York on Sunday 10 August was a repeat of the tumultuous welcome accorded by the city to the *Great Western* over seven years earlier. As before, crowds thronged the Battery and thousands gathered along the wharfs of the East River and the Brooklyn Heights to catch sight of the largest steamship in the world. The Americans were duly impressed by her size; *The New York Herald* used phrases such as 'a monster of the deep' and 'a sort of mastodon of this age'. The same writer nevertheless agreed that she was a magnificent vessel, and the general impression made on the population of New York was a distinctly favourable one—although there was some criticism of her rig which was thought to be unsightly compared with the tall and graceful masts of the square-rigged sailing barques of the Black Ball Line and other sailing vessels on Atlantic service.

The *Great Britain* remained in New York for nearly three weeks and the ship was open to visitors for most of that period. About a thousand a day went on board paying 25 cents for the privilege with a further 12½ cents to see round the engineroom. The return passage to Bristol was slightly shorter in duration by a few hours. The record of this voyage has survived and it is interesting to note the considerable variation in the distance covered on different days, the maximum being 287 miles on 8 September in contrast with only 160 miles two days earlier. On the former occasion the ship was probably running before a westerly wind fully rigged with sails while the shorter distance resulted from using the engines only. One of the advantages cited for screw propulsion was, of course, that it permitted the sails to be used more efficiently than when a ship was paddle-driven.

Nevertheless the performance of the vessel in terms of speed could only be described as moderate and it is obvious that the particular screw fitted was not as effective as had originally been hoped. There were other troubles as well, such as failure of the boilers to supply sufficient steam to the engines at all times, but these did not detract from the general impression that all would eventually be put right; then Robert Napier's prophecy of the triumph of steam over sail would be finally fulfilled on the transatlantic routes. The passengers on the first eastbound voyage certainly had no doubts about the future prospects of the *Great Britain*. Hosken was presented with an address by a group of leading passengers including several who were described as engineers. They were unanimous in recognising the advantages of iron in the construction of large ocean-going ships, and gave unqualified approval to the performance of the vessel, particularly her 'remarkable easy motion'. But they noted that the voyage could have been faster but for the 'shortage of steam power'. Hosken had previously been presented with a similar address on the outward voyage. This too commented on the lack of vibration which was considered to be less than in paddle vessels, so the driving gear with sprocketed chains must have performed tolerably well.

The second voyage to New York was far more eventful than the first. The ship was turned round as quickly as possible; it actually took 12 days, but this was a commendable performance considering the time required to load and trim, mainly by manual labour, nearly 1200 tons of coal. Her passenger list was longer this time—102 persons. The company must have felt that with one or two more successful voyages her reputation would be established, and even if she did take a day or so longer than the Cunard vessels, the spaciousness of her accommodation would continue to attract more and more passengers. The weather and fate in the form of a defec-

Crowds assembling on the Battery in New York to witness the arrival of the
Great Britain after her maiden voyage across the Atlantic

tive propeller however conspired to alter this feeling of confidence.
On the outward journey she was battered by gale force winds and
heavy seas during the first ten days, and in a squall on 2 October
her foremast was carried away. The high winds continued unabated
and she had to seek shelter on the American coast at Vineyard
Sound, south-east Massachusetts, for nearly half a day. Eventually,
after a further day waiting for the tide, she steamed into New York
early on 15 October; the voyage had taken 18 days. Three days
later she was moved into dry dock, where it was discovered that
two arms and one blade of her propeller were missing and almost
all the rivets were loose. It was decided to remove a further blade
to preserve the balance and tighten up the rivets in the hope that
this would be sufficient to get her back across the Atlantic to Liverpool—an unfortunate decision prompted by commercial pressures
on Hosken to complete each round voyage as quickly as possible.

The *Great Britain* left New York at 2 pm on 28 October and this
time there were only 23 passengers on board. The first sign of
further trouble with the screw came during the first watch on the
30th when part of the propeller appeared to be striking the stern
post very hard. Hosken immediately reversed the engines, and after
two or three further thumps the offending arm broke off. For two
and a half days she was able to make a reasonable speed with the
aid of the sails and then during the afternoon watch of 1 November
another propeller arm broke leaving only one and a half arms
attached to the central boss. The long apprenticeship under sail

served by Hosken and his officers now became invaluable. They proceeded under sail alone and despite being almost becalmed for several days they eventually reached the North West lightship off Liverpool at 8 pm on the 17th where the *Great Britain* anchored to wait for tugs and a pilot. The return leg had taken 20 days and it was obvious that there would be no quick turn round on this occasion. It was decided in fact to lay the ship up for the winter, and after discharging her cargo she went into the Queen's Graving Dock for an extensive refit.

Certain innovations that had been introduced to the rigging had not been very successful, though there had been little criticism of her sailing qualities. The opportunity was taken to fit manilla rope rigging in place of stranded iron wire, and at the same time the number of masts was reduced from six to five. This was done by removing the mast officially known as 'one', or 'Wednesday' in the vernacular of the crew. The main mast was altered to carry a main top mast and a top gallant mast instead of a single top mast as before. The mast known as 'two', situated about 20yd aft of the funnel, was similarly re-rigged and all masts were stepped at the kelson, like the main mast, instead of being hinged at the upper deck level.

There were three other major alterations. One of course was the fitting of a new screw. This time a four-blade design was adopted; the new screw weighed 7 tons, nearly twice as much as its predecessor although the diameter was the same as before—15ft 6in. It was made at the works at Bristol and taken up to Liverpool aboard the *Great Western* which had also been refitted during the winter. Another addition involved the fitting of two bilge keels 110ft long and 2ft deep, one on either side of the centreline to reduce rolling. In his original design Brunel had provided two lengths of angle iron on the keel, as described on page 57, and it is probable that these were used as the base on which to attach the bilge keels. The *Liverpool Journal* commenting on these alterations said that it was expected that her speed would be reduced by 2 knots, but this was not the case when she re-entered service. This was due to contract work carried out by a party of engineers from Maudslay Sons and Field. Every effort was made to increase the steam generating capacities of the boilers and improve the efficiency of the engines. The fire flues were enlarged, and the air pumps re-designed to increase the vacuum maintained in the condensers; adjustments were also made to the expansion valves. Indicator cards taken before and after these alterations showed a remarkable gain in the power developed by each cylinder. Where previously the mean effective pressure had been only 5.75lb/sq in, it was now 11.75

lb/sq in, and the output of the engines rose accordingly from 686 to 1663 ihp.

The *Great Britain* moved out of dock into the Mersey on the evening tide of 28 April and put to sea for 24 hours to test the new screw. The trials were satisfactory, the only incident being a near miss with a river steamer on her return to the Mersey. A disaster was in fact only narrowly averted by the fine seamanship of Hosken.

The first voyage in the new rig was almost as ill-fated as the homeward voyage in the previous October. There were only 28 passengers on board when she left Liverpool on 9 May although it was reported that she carried a large cargo. The journey again took 20 days but on this occasion it was a defective air pump that was responsible. The engines had to be stopped while a replacement part was made. This took six days, during which time the propeller was disconnected and the ship once again proceeded under sail alone. One is tempted to wonder if Robert Napier's recommendations regarding the carrying of engineroom spare gear were heeded aboard the *Great Britain*. When she did manage to use her engines again, it was only possible to steam at half speed—considerably slower than 11 knots that she had attained for a period under sail alone.

Permanent repairs were effected in New York and after a quick turn-round she sailed for Liverpool with 42 passengers on 8 June. She met adverse winds for most of the crossing but otherwise the voyage was uneventful and her machinery performed well. The passengers were full of praise for the comfort and sailing qualities of the vessel. The average distance covered on most days was about 230 nautical miles, the maximum being 280 and only on one day was the distance below 200 miles. The time taken was just over 13 days which was the quickest passage so far, although it was still longer than an average Cunard crossing and similar to the time taken by the *Great Western* on most of her sixty-four voyages. Nevertheless the directors must have felt that the teething troubles were over and that their luck had changed for the better.

This seemed to be confirmed on the fourth voyage when 110 passengers were booked on the outward journey. Again a good time was made. She left Liverpol at 9 pm on 7 July and arrived off Sandy Hook at midnight on the 20th. The voyage was not without incident as she ran into fog off the Newfoundland Bank and scraped a bilge keel on a reef off Cape Broil. Hosken could not have been too concerned as she was not docked for inspection until she returned to Liverpool when it was found that no damage had been sustained. On the homeward voyage one of the driving chains broke and this

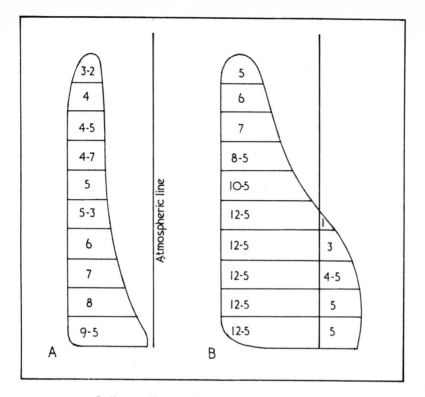

Indicator diagrams from an engine cylinder of the *Great Britain*. Diagram A was taken before the winter refit of 1845–6 when the mean effective pressure was only 5.75lb/sq in. Diagram B taken after the alterations shows a pressure of 11.75lb/sq in

took 18 hours to repair but the delay was made up, the total time on passage being once more a little over 13 days.

The examination in dry dock took place during the first week in September. Meanwhile bookings for the next voyage, which had been deferred until 22 September, continued to mount until they totalled 180, the highest number to date, not only for the *Great Britain*, but for any steamship on the Atlantic run. Even the more cautious members of the Great Western board must have felt that at last their gamble was going to pay off.

4 · Disaster at Dundrum Bay

Despite the proximity of the autumn equinox the weather was favourable when the *Great Britain* left Liverpool at 11 am on Tuesday 22 September. Hosken set a course that would take him south of the Isle of Man before turning to run up the Irish Channel and round the north of Ireland out into the Atlantic. Practically all her canvas was set and she made a good speed in the region of 13 knots. During the afternoon the weather deteriorated and when they passed the Calf of Man between 4 and 5 pm the visibility was very bad. Night set in, dark and wet, and as time wore on the conditions became progressively worse; the log was taken repeatedly and according to Hosken it showed only 11 knots. Suddenly at 9.30 pm there was a tremendous crash, the ship stopped abruptly and all confusion reigned. Some of the passengers believed they had hit another ship but Hosken realised they had gone aground. He admitted afterwards that he did not know where they were although he thought they might be near Ardglàss or Guns Island on the coast of Antrim. His first action was to go astern but the engineroom reported that the engines would not move.

Eventually it was found that they were aground at Dundrum Bay, a few miles to the south of Ardglass, although it was not until daylight that they discovered that they were only a little way to the west of the treacherous Cow and Calf rocks which had been the scene of many bad wrecks in the past. Once assured that the ship was in no danger of sinking, Hosken went below decks to reassure the passengers personally. It was decided that it would be too dangerous for the passengers to disembark that night, and some went calmly to their berths and slept until morning. For the majority, however, it was a truly unnerving experience and rest was out of the question. An indication of conditions on board was given in a letter by a lady passenger which was afterwards published in the *Illustrated London News* about a week after the wreck.

We have indeed been in fearful peril and the newspapers by no means represent the extent of the danger. All was confu-

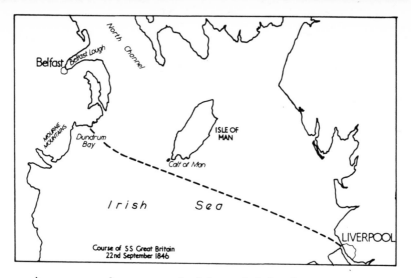

Course of SS Great Britain
22nd September 1846

sion; men and women rushed from their berths, some threw themselves into the arms of complete strangers; one could with difficulty stand. Mr. ———'s first words to me were 'I think there will be no loss of life but the ship is gone'.

What fearful words on such a dark night. Oh I cannot tell you of the anguish of that night! The sea broke over the ship, the waves struck her like thunder claps, the gravel grated below. There was the throwing overboard of coal, the cries of children, the groans of women, the blue lights, the signal guns, even the tears of men, and amidst all the Voice of Prayer, and this for long dark hours. Oh what a fearful night!

The day dawned and we lay between two long ledges of rock while another stretched across our front five hundred yards to right and left; the ship had been dashed to pieces. I cannot think of that night without tears but I feel and gratefully acknowledge the Hand of Merciful Providence was stretched out to protect and save us. The conduct of Captain Hosken through the night was admirable.

The unfortunate lady and her fellow passengers were taken ashore on Wednesday morning between 5 and 7 am. Their troubles were not yet over, as there were arguments with the local boatmen and carters who were assisting the disembarkation; most of the haggling ended amicably and agreement was reached regarding the luggage as well, but there were some passengers who refused to pay the sums demanded.

The mail was also unloaded and taken back to Liverpool in the packet boat *Sea King* for despatch to America by the next available boat. Some of the passengers travelled back in the *Sea King* and in a sister vessel *Maiden City* which docked at Fleetwood. The first news of the disaster was thus received in Liverpool on the morning of Thursday 24 September and a report appeared in *The Times* on the following day. This anticipated that the vessel would be refloated on the next spring tide which would be on 5 October.

More passengers returned to Liverpool on the steamer *Windsor* on the following day, and Gibbs, Bright and Co were besieged by those who wanted to continue their journey. All the passengers were full of praise for Hosken's conduct and said that they would be willing to re-embark in the *Great Britain* as soon as she was back in service. The company however wisely decided to refund their money and negotiations were started with Cunard for the sailing of the *Arcadia* to be advanced to take them to America. This however proved impossible, as it meant that Cunard would have to break the terms of the mail contract which involved a £500 penalty for every 12 hours delay.

Although no loss of life had occurred, the stranding of the *Great Britain* was a major tragedy for the Great Western Steamship Company. At first it seemed that she could be refloated without too much difficulty. There was no outward indication of damage to the hull, although the propeller and rudder had been bent. These facts were reported in a letter sent on 24 September by Captain Leonard Watson, the local Lloyds agent, who was one of the first outside experts on the scene. Work started on 25 September to lighten the ship by discharging a large part of the coal overboard and the rudder was straightened enabling the screw to be used. All stores were removed at this time and taken by tug to Liverpool. The work was hindered by a gale which blew from SSW all day on 26 September but there seemed to be every chance that the ship would be ready by the next spring tide. In the meantime three anchors were put out astern and two steam tugs with 90 fathoms of 9in rope were engaged to carry out the operation.

Captain Claxton arrived on 28 September. One of his first actions was to publicly thank the local people on behalf of the company for the assistance they had afforded to the passengers and crew on the morning after the wreck. He did this in a letter to the editor of *The Times,* and the fact that he took the trouble to write such a letter when there were many more urgent matters at hand is a favourable insight into his character. His presence must have been particularly welcome to Hosken as he immediately acquitted him of any blame. Speculation over the cause of the disaster had started almost as soon as the first passengers arrived in Liverpool. Many thought the compass was at fault, and one Canadian passenger reported that at the time of going aground he had seen an officer examining a compass which was not working properly and then going forward to check a second compass. Hosken, however, was adamant that neither the compass nor the steering gear had been defective, and he stated afterwards in his written report to the directors that he had checked all compasses on the day following the grounding and found them to be correct to within a quarter of a point.

He himself had no doubt as to the cause of the disaster. The fault lay with the chart which he had purchased in Liverpool in the previous June. The chart, which had been published earlier in the year by John & Alexander Walker, agents to the Admiralty, did not show a revolving or intermittent light on St John's Point at the entrance to Dundrum Bay, although the light had been in service since 1 May 1844. Hosken had steered for the Calf of Man and had calculated that his speed during the day was about 11 knots. Although he had caught a glimpse of the Isle of Man, as the weather thickened, he did not see the lights on the Calf and was afterwards confused by the appearance of a light on the starboard side which was not indicated on the chart. He admitted miscalculating the speed of the vessel and thought that this was probably due to the strong westerly drift.

Claxton took charge of the preparations for refloating the vessel; he was optimistic at first and predicted that she would be free in the first week of October. The crew continued with their herculean task of removing the coal with the aid of two iron funnels. It was a massive operation carried out under the most unpleasant conditions, as they eventually had to work up to their waists in water. On 3 October, the first attempt was made by two tugs the *Albert* and the *Dreadnought* but was unsuccessful; the only result was that her stern was moved round to a more favourable position. The weather deteriorated and further attempts that day were impossible. The crew, however, remained at their posts unloading the coal until it had all been taken ashore and carted away for sale.

The bad weather continued, and each successive high tide swung the ship round into a different position but was insufficient to float her off. This was perhaps not surprising, since one eye witness reported that part of the hull was embedded up to 5ft in the sand. Originally she had been pointing in a NE direction but by 6 October the bearing was WNW and ESE. The early optimism gave way to gloom. On 5 October it was reported that the rivets in the ship's bottom had started to leak and that there was 10ft of water in her hold. Claxton accepted then that she would not be refloated before the winter but refused to abandon her, despite a general feeling that she was doomed and would never be moved in a seaworthy condition. During the gales a heavy sea finally carried away the rudder and the propeller was further damaged by successive thumping on the sand. At high tide the sea was washing right over her, and Leonard Watson reported in a letter dated 9 October that the level was above the deck of the saloon. One eye witness considered that the only recourse was to haul her up the beach into a position where she could be conveniently broken up. The next gale however improved the situation to some degree, carrying her so far up the beach that she was left out of danger from the sea; her position was now NNW to SSE. A report in the *Liverpool Courier* said that Hosken actually set the sails to drive her up the beach—a desperate measure but a wise one in view of the fact that she was then making more than 2ft of water an hour above the capacity of the pumps.

The first phase of the salvage attempts was now over. Although they had been unsuccessful, the ultimate disaster had been avoided, and for the first time the idea of building a breakwater to protect her from the winter storms was considered. The directors sent William Patterson across from England to advise on its construction, and he was accompanied by Alexander Bremner, a salvage expert with a considerable reputation gained in reclaiming wrecks around the Scottish coasts. Bremner agreed that it would be unwise to attempt to move her until the spring. He assisted Patterson with the design of the breakwater, but both underestimated the force and fury of the autumn gales. The structure was built principally of logs; the cost was reported to be only £160 which indicates that it was not particularly large, even allowing that local timber and labour were used. Its useful life was in fact brief, since it was almost totally swept away in November.

Claxton, who was to remain in Ireland all through the winter, laboured heroically to prevent further damage to the ship, but despite many ingenious improvisations, the *Great Britain* still remained at the mercy of the weather like a stranded whale on an open beach.

The company inevitably received advice from all quarters on the methods to be adopted in floating off the vessel. Indeed the correspondence in *The Times* was almost evenly divided between those who proposed the most unpractical solutions to the problem, and those who sought to condemn Hosken, untried and unheard, for negligence. The directors requested Hosken to make a personal report which he prepared in writing on 13 October. He travelled across to Liverpool a few days later, calling first on Gibbs, Bright & Co to acquaint them with the latest developments, before proceeding to Bristol for his interview with the board. His account of the confusion caused by the faulty chart was accepted by the directors. He explained that since visibility was bad, he had chosen the northern route because there was less chance of encountering other vessels in unfavourable weather than on the southern route. He again admitted that he had miscalculated the speed and that he was not sure of their exact position when they went aground.

The board appears to have dealt humanely and perhaps even leniently with Hosken. The directors accepted his report and even endorsed his view that the primary cause of the disaster had been the omission of the St John's light from the chart. In a public statement they urged that heavy penalties should be exacted against all Admiralty agents who sold charts without a certificate proving that an annual check had been carried out on their accuracy by the Hydrographer's Department.

Hosken was never employed in the merchant service after the disaster at Dundrum Bay·but it would appear that this incident did not adversely affect his later career in the Royal Navy. He left the *Great Britain* in 1847 and was then appointed harbour master and chief magistrate in Labuan off north-west Borneo, a post that he held for two years. After service in the Mediterranian in command of a despatch vessel he was appointed to the hospital ship *Belle Isle* at the outbreak of the Crimean War and saw service in the Baltic and the Crimea. His promotion in the Royal Navy was steady if not spectacular; he retired with the rank of Captain in 1868, and was subsequently promoted to Vice-Admiral when on the retired list.

Hosken's report was published in full in *The Times* on 24 October. This led to a spate of letters under such pseudonyms as 'Nauticus', 'Trident' and 'Old Tar' which were mainly critical of Hosken's judgment. The writers certainly raised a number of pertinent questions, one of which sought an explanation why he had not altered course after land had been seen at 5.30 pm, as he had admitted in his report. No formal enquiry seems to have been held, and no doubt the directors of the company took into account Hosken's meritorious services in the past when they exonerated him from all blame. One source suggests that Brunel was not completely satisfied with the performance of the compass although it had been checked immediately after the grounding. In view of the evidence and the circumstances of the accident, it still seems a mystery why a master mariner in familiar waters should have found himself in this predicament, even allowing for the mistake on the chart and the poor visibility.

Public interest in the fate of the vessel remained high all through the autumn of 1846 and innumerable plans were put forward to secure her immediate release. The following letter written to the

Editor of *The Times* and published on 13 October is typical of several in which the good intentions of the writer are only exceeded by a lack of knowledge of marine salvage operations.

> Sir—In the different attempts to float the *Great Britain* nothing appears to have been done to buoy her up by placing airtight cases under her counters although the circumstances are by your accounts so peculiarly favourable for it as she is nearly high and dry at high water. A supply of old boilers might be had from Liverpool and even the vessel's own funnel secured at both ends would I should think help a great deal, as two or three feet more out of the water, aided by the high tides would float her.
>
> Your obedient servant,
> Suggestion.

An even more bizarre proposal came from Charles Macintosh, an inventor celebrated for a certain waterproof garment. As reported in *The Artizan* of December 1846, Macintosh suggested that an embankment should be built on the landward side against which should be secured open mouthed vessels directed at the ship containing waterproofed bags of gun powder. When fired these water cannon would create an immense wave which would roll seawards and carry the vessel with it.

Claxton and his fellow directors were probably too busy to pay much attention to all this gratuitous advice. They must have considered in their minds at least the possibility that the vessel would become a total wreck. Alarming rumours were already circulating that the underwriters would refuse to pay the insurance since the loss was due to gross negligence, and certain of the shareholders were also reported in the Bristol papers to be considering legal action as they believed that the vessel was considerably under insured—a figure of £18,000 was quoted when the cost of the vessel had been nearly £120,000. A glimmer of hope however came in the middle of November which did much to restore public confidence. This was the report of a survey carried out by an independent engineer named Billington who was positive that the vesssel could be refloated. Billington's brief had been merely to carry out a thorough examination, and he was not concerned with the salvage attempts. His report however, lacked the precision of one who knew the vessel intimately, and it was not until Brunel himself went to Dundrum Bay early in December that an accurate assessment of the damage to the engineroom was possible.

Brunel had been prevented from visiting the *Great Britain*

beforehand, first by the pressure of work on the South Devon atmospheric railway and secondly by Parliamentary business with which he was concerned. His feelings on seeing his great and splendid ship, lying virtually abandoned on this hostile shore, have been recorded in letters written successively to Claxton and the full board of directors.

'I was grieved to see this fine ship lying unprotected, deserted and abandoned by all those who ought to know her value and ought to have protected her instead of being humbugged by schemers and underwriters,' he complained to Claxton, and yet he was obviously relieved to find that no major structural damage had been sustained. He made a thorough examination of the machinery compartment where rocks beneath the ship had forced the boilers and both condensers bodily upwards. As a result the air pump associated with the forward condenser had been fractured, but this was the only item of machinery that had been seriously damaged.

Characteristically, Brunel immediately made a number of positive recommendations which he proceeded to act upon without waiting for the sanction of the Board. The main engines and air pumps were disconnected to prevent further damage as the ship was moved by the action of the tides. Secondly all strain was taken from the stern and a stream of water which washed sand away from her bottom was diverted. Most important of all were his recommendations for protecting the ship properly through the remainder of the winter.

I should stack a mass of large strong faggots lashed together, skewered together with iron rods, weighted down with iron, sandbags etc, wrapping the whole round with chains, just like a huge poultice under her quarters round under her stern, and half way up her length on the sea side.

In his report to the directors, which was subsequently printed and circulated to the shareholders, Brunel gave an indication of the various quantities of materials that would be required— 8 to 10,000 faggots, 3 to 400 fathoms of 1in or ¾in secondhand chain cable, 3 to 400 iron rods sharpened at the ends and 1,000 bags to fill with sand. It was obvious that a breakwater of this magnitude was going to cost far more than the £160 spent for the same purpose by Patterson and Bremner a couple of months earlier, but the directors adopted Brunel's proposals and Claxton was sent once more to Ireland to superintend operations. In the meantime, Hosken, who had returned to the ship at the end of October, had on Brunel's instructions assembled a gang of local labourers to collect the

Stranded at Dundrum Bay during the winter of 1846–7. The breakwater constructed by Claxton is shown in position protecting the after section of the vessel

bundles of faggots cut from the woods of the neighbouring estates. The construction of the breakwater went ahead without delay. It was a formidable task and the work was performed in appalling conditions. For days the thermometer dropped below zero and the men were lashed with icy winds which blew at near gale force across the open beach. At first it was difficult to establish a firm foundation, and despite all efforts to weight and lash the bundles down, the sea swept them away. With encouragement and admonishments from Brunel, Claxton and his men persevered, improvising and adapting their mode of working to overcome each problem as it was encountered. The foundations were laid at low tide, and each layer of faggots was pinned down with iron rods varying in length from 6 to 9ft. Stones and massive iron weights in the form of chains, air pump covers and even fire bars from the boilers were used to hold the fagggots in position as the tide swept in on the flood. The faggots themselves were quite substantial; they averaged 11ft in length and 5ft in circumference and were lashed together in bundles of varying numbers ranging from two to ten. One of the ship's iron lifeboats was also used in the foundations, being loaded with stones and forced down into the sand until only the gunwale was visible. Special emphasis was laid on protecting the stern and the breakwater was built up higher in the form of a large poultice to cover the exposed port quarter, as Brunel had recommended.

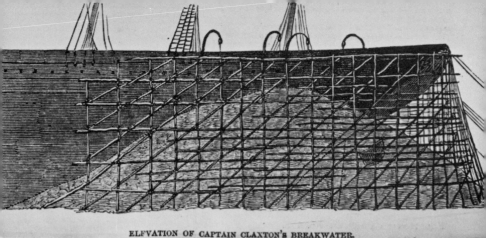

An engraving from the *Illustrated London News* showing details of the breakwater built at Dundrum Bay by Claxton to Brunel's specifications

Even when they had evolved a fairly satisfactory mode of working it was still a heart-breaking task, for parts of the structure collapsed periodically and had to be replaced. But it achieved its purpose and, although sections were swept away, the force of the waves on the ship's side was diminished. The 'green' wood used for the faggots in fact possessed a resilence which enabled it to give and then rebound after each onslaught of the advancing waves.

Claxton corresponded regularly with Brunel during this period and his letters, which were afterwards published, form a valuable record of the construction of the breakwater and the subsequent salvage operations. Early in March 1847, Claxton, on Brunel's suggestion, carried out some experiments with cork. It was thought that it might not be possible to block up the largest hole in the machinery space and Brunel proposed that both the engineroom and boiler room should be filled with cork to give the necessary buoyancy when she was floated off. Happily a party of boilermakers managed to stop most of the major leaks when the time came, so that the plan was never put into operation. The foreman boilermaker entrusted with this task was John Crew who was afterwards specially commended for making watertight six holes ranging from 2 to 6ft in length and up to 16in wide. Some of the holes were made deliberately soon after she had been stranded to admit the sea and hold her steady. Unfortunately about 300 tons of sand also accumulated in the various compartments and this had to be removed during February and March before salvage operations could be seriously attempted in the spring.

Claxton was hopeful that advantage could be taken of the high spring tides, and every effort was made to lighten the ship as far as possible, even to the extent of dismantling some of the machinery and shipping it across to Liverpool. It was all of no avail however; during the winter the scouring action of the tides had caused the ship to sink through the layer of sand and quarry a hollow in the rocks below. Some parts were embedded to a depth of 6ft in the sand and even the highest tide had no effect.

Early in May Claxton wrote to the company office suggesting that Bremner should be sent for again. Brunel supported this request and Bremner returned to Dundrum Bay on 22 May. He made a quick survey of the position and put forward a plan for lifting the vessel by means of spars with the aid of large boxes each containing 30 tons of sand. The boxes were to be suspended on tackles from the upper deck and moved up and down like the counter weight in a sash window. It was also proposed to use a series of levers acting on fulcra under the hull to give the initial impulse.

Bremner's scheme was simple in conception, but apart from sand which was on hand in abundance, it required various additional items that would take time to prepare. An estimate was submitted to the board for £460 0s 10d to cover the cost of labour and materials for the operation, and Claxton immediately set about ordering planks in order to make up the boxes. Patterson also arrived from Bristol during the latter part of May and his advice and experience proved to be of great assistance to Claxton, who continued to bear the chief responsibility for the conduct of the operation. Claxton also made many positive suggestions in the form of amendments to Bremner's plan which the latter was pleased to adopt.

Bremner had generously paid tribute to the effectiveness of Brunel's breakwater when he returned in May. The thoroughness with which it had been constructed was emphasised at the end of the month when work began to dismantle it so that the ship would have a clear passage to the open sea. By that time the faggots had become so compressed and the foundations were so tightly embedded, that Claxton felt that they would have had less difficulty had they been dealing with solid granite. Work continued simultaneously on the various aspects of the salvage operations, for Claxton was apprehensive about the weeks slipping past.

It was about this time that he was called to report on the position to both Houses of Parliament. Hitherto, although there had been widespread interest in scientific and nautical circles over the construction of the breakwater, the Government of the day had taken no direct action. Claxton was now invited to state what assistance he required and a Captain Williams of the Royal Engineers was sent over early in June to act as a liaison officer with the representatives of the company.

Bremner, aided by his son Alexander, continued through June to press on with the construction of his lifting apparatus and plans were made to attempt the raising and floating out on the high tides that were expected at the end of July. Some of the crew, who had been standing by the stricken vessel since the previous autumn, began to grow restive and eventually all but two of the seamen were discharged. There was also trouble from a group of carpenters who had been brought over from Bristol. They demanded exhorbitant rates of pay and were insolent to Bremner, but the strike which Claxton feared was averted. The press, sensing that the salvage operations were moving towards a climax, now re-appeared on the scene and *The Times* of 10 July reported that the fulcrum and levers on the outer side of the ship were finished. Claxton, using local labour, was busily engaged in filling the boxes with sand and hoisting them inboard at a rate of 50 tons a day. Holes were still being discovered in the hull even at this late stage, and Crew and his party were kept busy stopping the leaks.

Several unsuccessful attempts were made to refloat her during the middle of July, and another on 29 July when some progress was made. The ship was lifted bodily by Bremner's apparatus, and then wedged and shored up so that she could not sink back into her previous position in the sand. Two anchors were dropped about 900 yards away from the ship, positioned close together and connected with 450 fathoms of chain ready for hauling her off. Trouble continued between Bremner and the carpenters, and Claxton was glad of the return of Patterson once again since he could intercede between the two sides.

The Admiralty fulfilled their pledge to assist in the final salvage operations. The steam frigate *Birkenhead* arrived on 10 August and 56 riggers under the charge of a Mr Bellamy, the Assistant Master Attendant of Portsmouth Dockyard, together with 25 men from HMS *Victory* were landed in the ship's boat. On 14 August the *Birkenhead* tried to tow off the *Great Britain* single handed without success, and Claxton felt that more ships would be required. One problem which he anticipated, would be that of keeping the ship afloat after she had been finally towed off, and over thirty pumps were assembled on board for this purpose. They required over a hundred men to operate them, and a similar number to stand-by. Although additional seamen became available from HMS *Scourge,* which arrived during the third week in August, Claxton had to rely heavily on the local labourers who, as the climax approached, tended to make themselves scarce with the plea that they were required for the harvest. Every effort was made at this time to lighten the *Great Britain* as much as possible and the spare screw weighing 4 tons, which was still on board, was removed to the *Birkenhead.*

Another unsuccessful attempt was made on 26 August when the ship was moved about 5ft. Claxton, the two Bremners and Bellamy and his men laboured incessantly all day but with no avail. Undaunted they worked late into the evening to make further preparations for another attempt the next day. Time was getting short, for another equinox would soon be at hand, and Claxton must have realised that it was now or never. Bremner expressed his doubts that the ship would ever be salvaged, mainly on the grounds that the pumps would not be able to cope with the intake of water. Claxton, however, was adamant that a major effort should be made on the 27th and this time they were successful. Scarcely containing his elation Claxton wrote to Brunel that evening,

> Huzza, Huzza, you know what that means, I got more men at the pumps, Captain Fisher [the local coastguard officer in the Dundrum Bay area] came to my assistance with twenty coastguards, they worked on the large pumps splendidly and at one time she was drawn down four inches in half an hour showing that with good pumping we could even beat the leaks.

In his exuberance, Claxton omitted to mention that it was the pull exerted by the 600 hp engines of the *Birkenhead,* at 11.40 am, which finally released the *Great Britain* from her enforced captivity. One advantage gained from the previous attempts was that the crew knew what was expected from them, and one eye-witness reported that all orders were in the form of pre-arranged signals—not a word being spoken at the critical moments. A minor crisis arose when men were removed from the pumps to heave in the anchors and the ship nearly sank. Wisely, it was decided to leave the ship on the low tide mark that night and to examine the hull for any further leaks.

Arrangements were made for 120 men to man the pumps the next morning, but only 36 arrived at 8 am and these are reported to have spent most of their time haggling over money. Again the dockyard riggers and the men from the *Victory* stepped into the breach, and later in the morning the ship was moved out into deep water. Originally it was intended to tow her straight across to Liverpool, but despite herculean efforts at the pumps, water was gaining in the engineroom at a rate of 6in an hour. This was later reduced to 4in, but Claxton decided to make for Belfast. Towing the *Great Britain* was not an easy task for the *Birkenhead,* and the situation became hazardous when fog was encountered off the entrance to Belfast Lough. To make matters worse, the hawsers broke at a point where there was a strong current running, but boats were quickly lowered and fresh hawsers secured. Eventually the *Birkenhead* dropped anchor, and the *Scourge* towed the *Great Britain* inshore where she was deliberately grounded on the mud until the following morning. Claxton went ashore immediately and hired 200 labourers to assist in the floating off operations. Of this total 40 remained on board when the final stage of the journey to Liverpool began at 2 pm on the Sunday afternoon.

There was no lack of hands to man the pumps on this occasion, for in addition to the men hired at Belfast 50 members of the crew of the *Birkenhead* as well as the 56 riggers and 25 men from the *Victory* were also on board. The crew at this stage numbered about twenty-five so that altogether there were nearly three hundred available to cope with any emergency. The weather was favourable at first, and with the *Birkenhead* towing them as before they made about 6 knots. As they approached Liverpool, however, the wind freshened and there was trouble with the hawsers once again. First the starboard and then the port hawser broke. Both were quickly replaced, but the beam serving as a temporary rudder, which had been erected by the naval carpenters, gave way and fell overboard. Good seamanship all round prevented any further disaster happening. The men at the pumps laboured valiantly during the 23 hour crossing, and although she continued to make water the pumps were able to cope. Finally the *Birkenhead* handed over her charge to a tug, and at 1 pm on 31 August the *Great Britain* was manoeuvred into Princes Dock Basin, where she was greeted by a crowd as large as that which had cheered her off on her maiden voyage. Eye-witness reports say that her masts and rigging looked considerably worse for wear but the hull itself was not visibly damaged. Once in Princes Dock, the ship was manoeuvred over a gridiron onto which she sank and which supported her when the pumps were stopped.

A firm of ships' surveyors, Fawcett, Preston and Co, were immediately commissioned to survey the hull. The inspecting team were full of praise for the temporary repairs effected by John Crew and his team of boilermakers, and were unanimous that the hull was sound and that there was no evidence that any strain had occurred in the frames. This view was afterwards endorsed by John Grantham, who surveyed the vessel on behalf of the underwriters. The report from Fawcett, Preston and Co had wide circulation since it was included among the correspondence relating to the stranding—chiefly letters from Claxton to Brunel and the board—

that was subsequently published in book form. The surveyors ended their report with a significant statement in favour of iron as ship-building material. 'We do not conceive that it would have been possible under similar circumstances to stop holes of the size mentioned in the bottom of a wooden vessel; and we may further remark that the iron of which the frames and plates are made must have been of excellent quality.'

There was speculation in the press about the vessel's future, and the *Liverpool Albion* predicted correctly, as it transpired, that the engines and chain gearing would be removed. It was obvious that as the cylinders and other vulnerable components had been submerged at each high tide for months on end, they would have to be dismantled and each part thoroughly cleaned and examined, although any decision regarding repairs would depend upon the financial state of the company. For the present it was decided to stop up all the leaks, and then tow her to the south side of the Coburg Dock to wait upon events.

5 · Australia Bound

Although the salvage operations at Dundrum Bay were rightfully considered a great accomplishment (and Bremner proudly exhibited a model of his apparatus at the Great Exhibition in 1851) it was painfully clear to the directors of the GWSC that a considerable sum of money would have to be spent on the *Great Britain* before she could put to sea again. One estimate put the total at around £22,000—a sum that the company was in no position to pay, since the *Great Western*, their only source of revenue, had been sold to the Royal Mail Steam Packet Company for service between Southampton and the West Indies.

Eventually—there being no other alternative—it was decided to sell the *Great Britain* as well. Favourable reports from surveyors vindicating the use of iron may have been flattering to receive, but they had no effect on the company's balance sheet, and there was inevitably pressure from the more hard-headed members of the board that the company should cut its losses and go into liquidation. In April 1848, the ship's stores were auctioned at Liverpool. The occasion proved to be a field day for ships' chandlers and the local hoteliers, as vast quantities of bed linen, general furnishings and fittings all came under the hammer. Unsuccessful attempts were made to find a private buyer for the ship herself and so on 11 September 1848—just over five years after the launching which had been so full of great expectations—the *Great Britain* was ignominiously put up for sale in the Coburg dock. Messrs Tongue, Currie and Co, who conducted the auction, were instructed that the lowest acceptable price was £40,000 but the highest bid received was for only half that amount. In the circumstances it was felt by one or two observers that a bid of £35,000 or even £30,000 would have secured her but none was forthcoming.

She continued to remain in the Coburg dock for the next two and a half years, and during this time her future was the subject of much speculation. On 14 March 1849 *The Times* mentioned a rumour that the vessel had been sold for £25,000 to an unnamed company which proposed to operate a passenger service from the west coast of South America to San Francisco. The next report, which was equally without foundation, was that she had been bought by the Collins Line for £20,000, and that a further £22,000 was being spent to refit her once more for the North Atlantic service. E. K. Collins, the founder of the line bearing his name, took the trouble to write to the Editor of *The Times* on 23 June 1849 to refute this. A month later she was again put up for sale, but no realistic offers were made. Work was carried on during this period to dismantle those sections which were damaged, but a thorough refit could not be contemplated until a new owner appeared on the scene.

It was not until the end of 1850 that a satisfactory sale was made. At first it was reported that the new owner was none other than William Patterson, but it soon transpired that he was acting as the agent of Gibbs, Bright and Co. The price was a mere £18,000— less than one sixth of her original cost. It was rumoured that the ship would be used to bring visitors from the USA to the Great Exhibition of 1851, but in view of the vast amount of work required to put her back into service it is unlikely that this was ever seriously contemplated.

After the sale of the *Great Britain* was completed the GWSC was wound up in February 1852. Details of the final balance sheet are given in an appendix on page 128. Another company with the same name but with no connection was incorporated in 1881 to carry on business as shipowners and ship and insurance brokers. Offices were opened in Bristol, Avonmouth and New York and a capital of £1,000,000 was raised. This was also an unfortunate venture and the company ceased business in 1895.

Gibbs, Bright and Co had interests in the USA, Canada, the Far East and Australia. They were founded in the early years of the nineteenth century, and the company had prospered with the general increase in British overseas trade. They also had strong commercial connections in both Bristol and Liverpool.

The new owners were determined not to pay dock dues any longer than was necessary, and work began in earnest to prepare the ship for sea. She was moved to the Shandon Graving Dock and a local firm of shipwrights, Messrs F. Vernon and Son, were engaged to make the necessary repairs to the interior of the hull. Soon about 150 workmen were employed on the contract. The remnants of the original engines and the gear drive were removed, and alterations were made to the structure of the hull. The bottom plates amidships over a length of 150ft were renewed and many of the deck supporting frames in the lower part of the ship were strengthened with additional lengths of angle iron. The bow and stern were also

The *Great Britain* as she first appeared under the flag of Gibbs, Bright and Co in 1852. Her masts were now reduced to four and twin funnels were fitted athwartships

reinforced by the addition of double angle iron framing secured by three tiers of iron stringers 2ft 3in wide and $\frac{5}{8}$in thick, which were riveted to the framework at right angles. Ten iron kelsons were arranged to run the whole length of the ship fore and aft; these were half as deep again as those formerly employed. Box kelsons 3ft 6in deep and fabricated from $1\frac{1}{4}$in iron plate were installed in the engineroom to support the new engines and boilers. Basically the hull design remained unaltered, it was simply strengthened in the more vulnerable places, and a thorough examination conducted of the framing and plates.

The policy of the new owners was to obtain as much cargo space as possible, and to achieve this the ship was transformed into an auxiliary screw steamer. Smaller engines and boilers were fitted and a deckhouse running nearly the full length of the ship was built on top of the original upper deck. The original saloon was now to serve as a cargo space, and it was estimated that a further 1,000 tons would be carried as a result of these alterations. The new saloon in the deckhouse was as spacious as the one it had replaced and could accommodate 200 passengers. The alterations at the upper deck level also included the removal of the iron rail which had previously extended right round the ship and its replacement by a wooden bulkhead 4ft 6in high. All the work relating to the upper part of the ship including the new deckhouse was undertaken by Messrs Mackay and Miller.

By August 1851, it was reported that 350 men were working on the vessel under the overall supervision of William Patterson—the only member of the original building committee now directly

associated with the ship. The scene at the Shandon dock now
resembled that at the Wapping Dock in Bristol seven or eight years
earlier; a small steam engine was erected in a shed near the dock
to drive drilling machines, punching presses and grind stones, and
the work was carried out with a sense of urgency that led one
observer to predict that the *Great Britain* would be back in service
before the end of the year.

A fair proportion of the labour force was concerned with the
installation of the new boilers and engines. The boilers were described as operating on the 'tubular principle', each of the six
boilers having 280 brass tubes and three furnaces. All the boilers
were arranged separately and were identical in size, measuring 11ft
long, 9ft wide by 13ft high. They were built by John Penn and
Son of Greenwich, who were also responsible for the engines. The
working pressure was 10 lb/sq in, and it is possible that they may
have been an early version of a water-tube boiler, since Penn is
known to have fitted this type of boiler as early as 1842 in a number
of small steamboats for service on the Thames.

John Penn also took out several patents for marine steam engines,
notably No 11017 on 23 December 1845 and No 12386 on 21
December 1848, and it is probable that the new set of engines
was based on one of these patents. They were oscillating in design
—a type of engine for which Penn was justly famous. They comprised two cylinders, each having a diameter of 82½in and a stroke
of 6ft. The cylinders were arranged fore and aft on the centreline
of the engineroom and drove an overhead crankshaft. This was
similar to the arrangement of the original engines except that there
were only two cylinders instead of four. There was, however, a
fundamental difference in the method of transmitting power to the
propeller shaft. Brunel's four massive chains were dispensed with,
and a relatively simple gear drive was adopted. The main gear
wheel on the crankshaft had four rows of teeth, which engaged in
similar teeth on a small pinion below, located at the inboard end
of the propeller shaft. The ratio of the gears was exactly 3 : 1. The
wrought iron propeller shaft was in four sections which together
totalled 105ft with the couplings it weighed 24 tons. The engines
were smaller than those originally fitted, being only 500 nominal
hp. They drove, initially, a 3-bladed cast iron propeller with
a diameter of 15ft 6in and a pitch of 19ft.

Alterations were also made to the rigging and the masts were
now reduced from five to four. The second and third masts carried
square sails, and the third mast which was aft of the funnels was
designated as the main mast since it was the taller of the two. The
other masts were still schooner rigged, and the ship was described

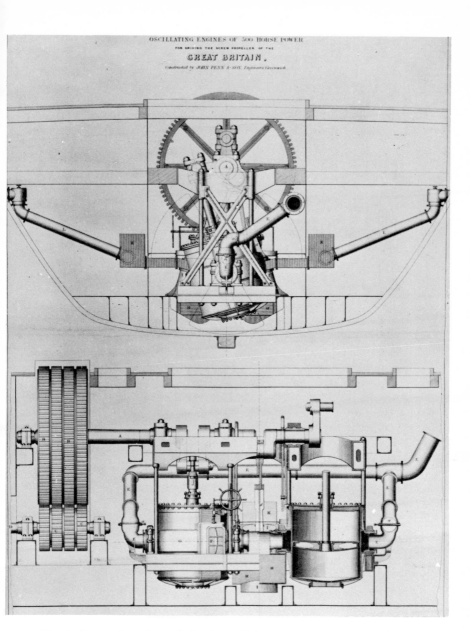

The boilers and engines of the *Great Britain* after the reconstruction at Liverpool 1850-52. A twin cylinder oscillating engine patented by John Penn was installed and power was transmitted to the main shaft through a simple gear drive

as such when she was registered. The two funnels were a distinguishing feature since they were placed side by side athwartships, and each served three boilers.

It was during the summer of 1851, while the reconstruction work was progressing with all speed, that a new captain was appointed to the *Great Britain*. The man selected was Captain Barnard Matthews who had previously been in command of the *Great Western* and the *City of Glasgow*. Captain Matthews was to spend many months on board getting familiar with the ship before he was able to take her to sea on trials. The original estimate for the completion date was hopelessly optimistic, and it was not until 22 March 1852 that the *Great Britain* eventually left the dockside at Liverpool. The news that she was on the move at last was sufficient to cause a large crowd to assemble at a number of vantage points, and she was cheered down river once again. The reception must have been appreciated by those on board who had been responsible for the alterations, notably Samuel and Tyndall Bright for the new owners, John Penn and Vernon, the shipwright. Also on board for these second trials were Francis Smith and Christopher Claxton, who had both been intimately connected with the first series of trials in the Bristol Channel. Four and a half years had elapsed since the *Birkenhead* had towed the partly flooded *Great Britain* across the Irish Sea and it must have been a proud moment for Claxton, tinged perhaps with nostalgia, as the vessel slipped down the Mersey with the house flag of Gibbs, Bright and Co at the mainmast instead of that of the GWSC.

Brunel was not present on this occasion. His official connection with the ship would have ceased a few weeks earlier when the GWSC finally went into liquidation. There is little evidence to show whether he had any influence on the vessel's future once she was towed back to Liverpool and it is unlikely, with the enormous demand for his services as Chief Engineer of the GWR, that he could have devoted much time to the ship during the years 1848-52. Undoubtedly, he reassured himself by personal inspection that she did have a future, but he probably realised that the role which this would take would be determined by economic forces beyond his control. In 1852, when the *Great Britain* was beginning the second phase of her career, he was already drawing up plans for his third great ship—the *Great Eastern* which would dwarf his earlier vessels many times over. Thomas Guppy was another notable absentee. He had accepted the post of manager of the Cwmavon Copper Works in 1845, but four years later moved to Italy where he practised as a civil and mechanical engineer.

The trials, on which so much depended, took place almost without

Leaving Liverpool on 21 August 1852 for the first voyage to Australia

incident. The *Great Britain* left the river at noon in company with the steam packet *Admiral* which was on passage to Le Havre. By about 12.45 pm she was off the Crosby lightship and was about ¼ mile ahead of the *Admiral*. The engines were then making 18 rpm after which the topsails were set and her speed increased to 11 knots. At 1.10 pm she passed Bell Buoy with the *Admiral* ½ mile astern, and by 2.30 pm she was abreast of Rhyl. It was then that the main bearings ran hot, and she stopped for about ½ hour while adjustments were made. Thereafter the engines behaved perfectly, and a course was set for Holyhead where she arrived at 6 pm after covering 70 miles in 5 hours 40 minutes. Samuel Bright and his party were landed at Holyhead, but the ship remained at sea for nearly another 48 hours to test all the machinery as thoroughly as possible. A sustained full power run was carried out, during which the designed maximum speed of 10 knots on engines alone was maintained for a period of 10 hours. It was reported afterwards, almost as an afterthought, that the compasses behaved perfectly. This was probably to reassure a small minority of sceptics, who still harboured doubts about the effect of an iron hull on compass performance. But as more and more iron ships came into service during the 1850s even the most conservative ship owners realised that, provided the necessary adjustments were made, there could be no criticism regarding the use of iron in this respect.

Gibbs, Bright and Co decided initially to employ the *Great Britain* on the transatlantic run, and berths were advertised for the second 'maiden' voyage to begin on 1 May 1852. The response was encouraging; 180 passengers and a considerable tonnage of cargo were on board when she sailed from Wellington Dock at 9.10 am on Saturday, 1 May. The voyage began well; she steamed the first 13 miles to Bell Buoy in an hour and the absence of vibration was soon noticed by the more experienced passengers. There was general approval of the refurnished saloon, particularly the 75ft long Grand Saloon on the after part of the main deck, that was decorated with various national shields painted on glass. The provision of a music room, smoking room and separate ladies' boudoirs also received favourable comment. The time taken on passage to New York was 13 days 5½ hours, which was satisfactory but not spectacular. Captain Matthews drove the ship hard, and with a good following sea covered 301 miles on 12 May which was, up to that time, the greatest distance steamed by a screw-driven ship in 24 hours. Matthews, like Hosken before him, made a good impression on the passengers and duly received the customary testimonial address at the end of the voyage.

With their extensive interests in Australasia and the Far East, it was not surprising that the new owners announced in June that the *Great Britain* was being transferred to the Eagle Line, one of their subsidiary shipping interests, and would henceforth operate a service between England and Australia. It is possible that they may have assessed their chances of competing effectively against Cunard on the North Atlantic as slim, but there were a number of positive reasons for switching routes. Gold had been discovered at Bathurst, New South Wales, in 1851, an event which immediately led to a tremendous upsurge in emigration from Britain. There was an unprecedented demand for shipping berths, and the company concluded that their auxiliary screw flagship would be ideal for this purpose.

There had been speculation concerning the establishment of a regular steamship service between England and Australia for several years. In 1846, a select committee of the New South Wales Legislative Council examined a number of proposed routes. They were in favour of making the journey in relatively short stages via the Cape, India, Singapore and down the East coast of Australia, with suitable coaling stations at each major port of call. The more direct route from the Cape across the Southern Indian Ocean to Adelaide was ruled out, as it was thought it would be impossible for a ship to carry sufficient coal to steam the distance of 6100 miles.

It is likely that the committee visualised vessels of perhaps a 1000 tons burden being employed on this service but the increased demand for passages now made it possible to use a ship the size of the *Great Britain* with a correspondingly greater coal capacity. News of her transfer to the Australian run led immediately to a large number of bookings, and a total of 650 passengers were on board when she sailed from the Mersey at 3 pm on Saturday 21

August to begin what was to be the most satisfactory stage in her career.

Once again vast crowds assembled to watch her passage down the Mersey. All river craft, including the local steam ferries, were dressed overall for the occasion and the cheering was punctuated by the booming reports of the *Great Britain*'s saluting guns. Gibbs, Bright and Co had reason to congratulate themselves on the number of berths sold. With 70 gns for an upper saloon berth, 40 gns for a forward saloon berth and 25 gns for a second class cabin, they could expect to recover fairly soon at least a portion of the capital invested in the ship's reconstruction.

One of the features of the second phase of the *Great Britain*'s career is that a great deal more is known about the day-to-day life of the passengers than is the case with the earlier voyages to New York. This is no doubt due to the greater duration of the voyages which encouraged the literary minded to keep diaries and even produce ship's newspapers to relieve the tedium of the long days at sea. Several of the ship's journals or papers have survived and provide a wealth of information about the social habits of Victorian travellers. A description of part of the first voyage to Australia was published in *The Times* of 13 November 1852 in the form of extracts from the diary of a saloon passenger. The writer seems to have been excessively preoccupied with the ambient temperature at various latitudes as the following passages show but he has given a fascinating glimpse of the daily routine.

21 August—Liverpool. At 4 p.m. the last steamer left us
22 August—Sunday. At 11 a.m. Captain Matthews read the service, crew too busy to attend—saloon crammed. At 9 p.m. service again. At 11 p.m. went over the ship. Thermometer low in second class cabins as in my own berth. The Captain has a great deal of tact with his passengers, his manner and arrangements on Sunday made a great impression on us all
23 August—J. Clark, a second cabin passenger reports he is robbed of £35. At night singing and dancing on deck
24 August—Clark finds his money. Other passengers wanted to duck him but Captain Matthews interfered. Passengers deposit several sums of money with Cox (1st Mate)
25 August—After saloon passengers pleased with fare. Whist, music, Shakespeare readings, chess, draughts, in saloons, dancing, singing. In the fore saloon there are many passengers who seem well able to pay for aft saloon berths. I think they seem to expect more than what they got for what they pay—£44. 11 p.m. Second cabins same temperature as aft saloon

26 August—Steaming ten miles an hour

27 August—Disconnected the screw but it takes a 10 knot sailing breeze to beat the engines

28 August—Weather warmer. Thermometer—aft saloon berths 76 deg, midship 81 deg, fore saloon 72 deg, second cabin forward 75 deg, aft 80 deg.

29 August—Passed Palma, distance about 4 miles. At 1 a.m. squall and a bright moon

30 August—Weather hot and all less inclined to do anything. At 11 p.m. thermometer aft saloon 80 deg, fore saloon 80 deg, second cabin aft 79 deg, forward 82 deg. The notices on the mainmast were as follows : By permission from Captain Matthews a Sunday school for children will be commenced next Sunday 29 August, hours 3 to half past 4. Parents are invited to send their children and the assistance of ladies as teachers is requested. Found at 4 p.m., a silver watch—apply to the Chief Officer. Divine service will commence at 10.30 a.m. : all passengers are requested to attend. The secretary has prevailed upon the following gentlemen to take the management of the readings of Scott, Dickens, Shakespeare etc and trusts the passengers will give them their cordial support (names)

1 September—Stewards have hard work, 2040 plates have to be washed, 2720 cups and saucers, 900 knives, 900 forks etc

2, 3, 4, 5 September—Nothing worth mentioning

6 September—Sunday Service at 10.30 a.m. and 8 p.m., saloon crowded

7 September—Was asked to dine in fore saloon by a passenger; had a capital dinner. At 9 p.m. Neptune and his satellites came on board and shaved all the new ship's company and myself. Nothing worth mentioning till—

14 September—Jews, 13 on board, held a synagogue in officer's messroom

16 September—Blowing fresh. All very much excited about a ball or concert to be given today. Wind has increased and night rough and stormy

17 September—Wind ahead, blowing hard. S.E. heavy sea, ship rolling and pitching very much; one of the sails for'ard blown away

18 September—Blowing hard and heavy sea; no one could sleep, very heavy seas continually striking the vessel. Captain Matthews put the ship round for St Helena to take on more coal

19 September—Sunday. Service at 10.30 a.m. and 8 p.m.

20, 21 September—Going before the wind, expect to be in St. Helena by Wednesday night; all comfortable, the detention will be a greater loss to the owners than to ourselves

22 September—Running before the wind fresh from S.E. and occasionally very squally

23 September—Wednesday, Blowing very fresh, ship going 8 knots with screw disconnected. At 10 p.m. connected screw again, health officers came aboard. In four days it is expected we shall be off again.

It seems obvious that there had been a miscalculation in the amount of coal required to reach the Cape even though most of the voyage down to the southern latitudes was under sail alone. Colliers were sent out to Cape Town in advance to await the arrival of the *Great Britain;* and the ship herself was supposed to have been well bunkered with Welsh steam coal, as well as carrying a small quantity of anthracite, and some experimental patent fuel of unknown description. After refuelling at St Helena she proceeded on her way to the Cape without further incident. Fresh meat in the form of livestock was taken aboard at Cape Town, from whence she sailed on 17 October. The long voyage to Melbourne, mostly in the 'roaring forties' was uneventful and the ship arrived in Port Phillip Bay on 12 November, thus making the passage from Liverpool in 82 days.

Melbourne gave the *Great Britain* a tumultuous welcome but she remained in the port only a few days before leaving for Sydney. A number of extra passengers joined the ship for the last leg of journey. Unbeknown to Captain Matthews, these included many undesirable characters who had been declared *persona non grata* in the colony of Victoria. Apparently they must have behaved themselves, as there was no report of any trouble when the ship arrived in Sydney on 20 November and anchored in Neutral Bay. The owners' agents in Sydney were then known as Bright Brothers and Company although the name was subsequently altered to Gibbs, Bright Pty Ltd. They were evidently as shrewd as their principals in Liverpool since they opened the ship to the public at 5s a head to take advantage of the tremendous interest in the vessel—the like of which had never been seen before in Sydney Harbour.

The ship's officers were liberally entertained ashore, and the hospitality they had received was reciprocated when a dance was held on board before the *Great Britain* returned to Melbourne. She left Port Phillip on 6 January 1853 homeward bound with 260 passengers on board and a cargo principally of wool, but which also included 135,000 oz of gold dust to the value of £550,000. There was also a large quantity of gold held privately by the passengers in amounts estimated to vary between £150-£2000 a man. These were the successful diggers who had struck it rich, and were returning to the 'Old Country' to enjoy their new-found wealth. Their number also included several enterprising gentlemen who had made fortunes without going near the gold fields, such as an ex-Melbourne publican who had made £20,000 in 10 months, and a former circus owner whose profit in similarly short space of time amounted to £30,000. No doubt they were all doubly impatient to enjoy the fruits of their labours by the time they arrived in Liverpool on 2 April after a voyage of 86 days, of which 72 had been spent at sea. The *Great Britain* had again suffered from a shortage of coal, despite topping up the bunkers at Simon's Bay near Cape Town—an operation which took eight days and suggests that they must have been nearly empty on arrival. To conserve coal only four boilers were used, and the designed maximum speed of 10 knots was only maintained for twenty-four hours on one day only. She was long overdue when she entered the Mersey, and her now customary tumultuous welcome was accompanied by feelings of profound relief.

Modifications were obviously necessary to improve the efficiency of her boilers. The work was put in hand as soon as possible and at the same time the opportunity was taken to alter her rigging once again. Another mast was removed, thus reducing the total to

The *Great Britain* in Sydney Harbour, December 1852. The public were permitted on board at 5s a head to inspect the ship

During further alterations in 1853 her masts were reduced to three and
a single funnel replaced the twin funnels amidships

three which were now all square rigged. This gave her, in the words
of one writer, a very majestic appearance resembling that of a large
steam frigate. Another major alteration to her silhouette was that,
as result of the changes to the boilers, a single funnel was erected
in place of the twin funnels athwartships. Finally, a two-blade
screw patented by Robert Griffiths was fitted in place of the
3-bladed cast iron screw.

The refit was carried out remarkably quickly and on 11 August
1853 the *Great Britain* left Liverpool on her second voyage to
Australia. On this occasion there were 364 passengers on board
comprising 84 first class who now paid 72 gns for their berths, 119
second class at 42 gns and 161 at varying prices from 25-32 gns.
She also carried 600 tons of cargo at an average rate of £8 per ton
and 1400 tons of coal. Only private mail was on board since Gibbs,
Bright and Company decided not to tender for the mail contract
which was only £1000 per trip. On the outward journey, she called
at St Vincent for more coal, and made good time to Melbourne
arriving on 16 October, the passage taking 67 days. She went on to
Sydney and returned to England round the Horn for the first time,
coaling at the Falkland Islands, where a stock of coal had been
built up chiefly for her use. Again the time was satisfactory, the
return voyage being accomplished in 63 days, which indicates that
the modifications of the previous summer had been successful.

A change in command took place after the second voyage to
Australia. Captain Matthews retired and recommended that his
successor should be John Gray, a remarkably young man of thirty-

four who had joined the ship as second mate two voyages earlier. The company appointed Gray but prevailed upon Matthews to make one more round voyage with the rank of superintendent. John Gray, a Shetlander, was a distant relative of Arthur Anderson, the founder of the P & O line. He was to become the most celebrated of all captains of the *Great Britain* and held the post until his death fourteen years later. A man of outstanding character and ability, he began his career under sail, and achieved command of his own ship while in his early twenties. A chance meeting in Liverpool with an old acquaintance led to the offer of a position on the *Great Britain* as second mate. He made one voyage before being promoted first mate, and again only one voyage before Captain Matthews recommended that he should succeed him. Gray's tenure of command began with a minor mishap, for the *Great Britain*'s screw was damaged soon after she left Liverpool on 28 April 1854. She had to return for repairs and finally left again on 13 June. It was during this voyage in July 1854 that the ownership of the *Great Britain* was formally transferred to the Liverpool and Australian Navigation Company. Gibbs, Bright and Co continued to act as managers and Tyndall Bright was the secretary.

The gold rush in the Colony of Victoria was now at its height, and it was reported that there were more than a 1000 passengers on board who had paid 25 gns each. The voyage was apparently free of incident until smallpox broke out, causing the ship to be quarantined on arrival off Port Phillip on 15 August. The authorities refused to let her proceed beyond Portsea, and stationed an armed cutter near by to ensure that the quarantine regulations were observed. Gray was placed in an awkward situation with hundreds of frustrated diggers on his hands, but he avoided trouble by putting the crew and passengers to work ashore building a temporary camp. One smallpox victim died, but the epidemic was arrested and on 6 September the port medical officer visited the camp and gave everyone a clean bill of health.

The *Great Britain* had meanwhile been well fumigated by burning sulphur between decks, and as soon as all passengers and crew had returned aboard, she raised steam and proceeded up Port Phillip Bay. There she received her customary welcome from ships anchored off Williamstown and Sandridge (now Port Melbourne), and responded in her usual manner by firing her saluting guns. These may have been fired with slightly more abandon than was normally the case to celebrate the release from quarantine, as several other ships replied and added to the noise with flares and salvage rockets. It was a harmless display of pyrotechnics, as far as the sailors were concerned, but to the citizens of Melbourne a few miles from the shore the sound of cannon from the Bay with the glare of flares overhead implied something very different. The city had been full of rumours since the outbreak of the Crimean War, to the effect that a Russian fleet was on its way to invade Australia. The booming of cannon in the distance was all that was needed to send the more jittery-minded citizens into a panic. Two regiments of infantry were called out supported by hundreds of volunteers who had previously been organised to defend the colony. Fortunately before any shots were fired in earnest the Governor, Sir Charles Hotham, despatched the Colonial Secretary, Captain William Lonsdale, to the shores of Port Phillip Bay to report on the situation. Lonsdale prudently sought out the harbour master and, on learning the true explanation of the cause of the noise, was able to prevent the military and their accomplices from firing on their fellow countrymen. The 'invasion of Melbourne' was over before it had started, although it remained a topic of conversation in the bars of the city for many months afterwards.

The *Great Britain* herself was to be far more closely involved in the Crimean War, for her owners agreed that she should serve as a troop transport on her return from her third voyage to Australia. She was prepared for this task in the late winter of 1854-55 and her accommodation was altered and enlarged. It was reported in the *Illustrated London News* of 3 March 1855 that she could carry 1500 men and 56 officers, and to accomplish this a total of 1359 hammocks and 162 berths had been provided. She was victualled for ten weeks and a full quota of medical supplies was carried. She sailed on 7 March, and for the next ten months was continuously employed in the Mediterranean and Black Sea, during which time she transported some 44,000 British and French troops to and from the war zone.

At the end of her Crimean service it was necessary to give her an extensive refit, refurnishing her passenger accommodation and restoring her cargo hold to its original size. Her machinery was thoroughly overhauled, her masts and yards were again enlarged and a poop deck, 104ft long, was constructed. This work took upwards of nine months, and it was not until 15 February 1857 that she resumed her service to Australia. She made only one round trip however before she was once more involved with the needs of the military—this time to take troops to India to reinforce the garrisons who were attempting to quell the Indian Mutiny. On 8 October 1857 she embarked the 17th Lancers, the 8th Hussars and part of the 56th regiment of infantry at Cork and sailed for Bombay, arriving there on 17 December. After just over a month, she returned via Table Bay and reached Liverpool on 10 April 1858.

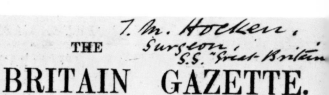

T. M. Hocken,
Surgeon,
S.S. "Great Britain"

THE
GREAT BRITAIN GAZETTE.

Vela damus vastum que

cavâ trabe currimus æquor.

No. 1.   SATURDAY, JULY 6, 1861.   PRICE 6D.

THE LAND WE'VE LEFT BEHIND US.

Various are the reasons which have induced the five or six hundred individuals congregated together in the good Ship GREAT BRITAIN, to leave the land of gold. Some, doubtless, are for visiting and taking a last farewell of the "old folks at home." Some on business. Some, perhaps, to take a wife unto themselves. Others may have "made their pile :" and not a few (judging from the tenor of their converse,) are "thoroughly disgusted" with the "land of promise." Hence we have within ourselves a fruitful source of discussion, which, if carried out in a right spirit, is calculated to edify as well as enlighten the minds of those who desire to "live and learn."

The "fourth estate" having come forward to the rescue of those who were famishing through lack of literary food, an fine opportunity is presented for the expression of opinion on the subject—"Is Victoria or England the best place for the working man ?" Believing there is sufficient talent on board to handle the subject in a fair and intelligible manner, I merely throw out the hint, with the hope that it will be taken up in a friendly manner, and conclude by promising to prepare an article on the subject for your Second Number ; and further, I beg to inform your readers that I purpose endeavouring to prove that, for the working man, Victoria is preferable to the British Isles.

E. E. M.

The front page of 'The Great Britain Gazette'. Published on board during a homeward voyage from Melbourne to Liverpool via Cape Horn

The Eleven of All-England who travelled out to Australia in the *Great Britain* in October 1861. This was the first English cricket team to visit Australia

intemperate minority who spent much time in the ship's bar. A pamphlet published in Melbourne in 1866 by a disgruntled ex-passenger gives an insight into the more seamy side of life during an outward voyage, with a sprinkling of remittence men and other social misfits on board. Entitled 'The Adventures and Sufferings of an Old Colonist on board the *Great Britain*' it consisted mainly of a diatribe by the author against certain of his fellow passengers although it also included a generous tribute to Gray's all-round competence.

Dealing with recalcitrant passengers must have been only one of the Captain's problems, for the *Great Britain* was not an easy ship to handle when under sail, and taking in sail when a storm blew up called for seamanship of the highest order. On such an occasion the mate would take charge of the foremast, the second mate the mainmast and Gray, with the aid of the carpenter would handle the mizzen. Since the masts, yards and sails were of such gigantic proportions great difficulty was often experienced, particularly when reefing the topsails. On one occasion fifty men, twenty-five on each side of the mast, tried to take in a reef in the foretopsail during a gale, but eventually the attempt was abandoned.

Gray disappeared at sea in mysterious circumstances on a homeward voyage from Australia. There was a suspicion of foul play in view of the large sums of money kept in his cabin, but he had also been suffering from the effects of malaria contracted on the previous voyage. He was alone in his cabin, but when it was next visited Gray had vanished and the porthole was found open.

For a number of years afterwards the *Great Britain* continued on the Australian run and some of her fastest passages were made during this period. In 1873 she took only 57 days on the outward voyage on two occasions, although the record remained at 55 days, accomplished under Gray's command in 1860. During the 1870s it became apparent, however, that she was no longer able to compete economically with vessels fitted with compound engines, and finally on 1 February 1876 at the completion of her thirty-second voyage to Australia, she was withdrawn from service and laid up at Birkenhead.

This was to be the end of her career as a steamship although it was not realised at the time. Penn's oscillating engines had served her well but they were now grossly outdated compared with the four cylinder compond engines—two high pressure and two low pressure cylinders—that were being installed in vessels built for the P & O and other established shipping companies. The decisive decade in marine engine development was the 1860s, when the theories of Thompson and Rankine were translated into practice by men like John Elder and Edward Humphrys. Steam pressures that were six or seven times as high as those used in the *Great Britain* became common, and this led to vastly improved thermal efficiencies, with a corresponding reduction in coal consumption. Eventually, it became possible to steam to Australia all the way, and the days of the sailing vessels and, similarly the auxiliary screw steamer, were numbered.

By 1876 however, and indeed for some years previously, it had been abundantly clear that the combination of iron hull construction and screw propulsion was the pattern for future development, and that the ships of the newly created steam navy and the rapidly expanding merchant marine were the linear descendants of the

A photograph taken at Gravesend in 1875—towards the end of her service between England and Australia. Then over 30 years old she was still among the smartest ships afloat

Great Britain, as conceived by Brunel. Acceptance of the superiority of iron and of screw propulsion had not come overnight. Cunard, who admittedly were hampered by Admiralty restrictions mentioned on page 58, did not sanction the use of iron until 1855, when the *Persia* was built by Robert Napier, who adopted many of Brunel's innovations to ensure maximum longitudinal strength of the hull. Many engineers, including Napier, also continued to insist on the superiority of paddles. There was much evidence to support this view, even as late as 1862 when Napier designed the *Scotia* for Cunard, which was the last paddle-driven vessel to hold the Blue Riband of the Atlantic. Improvements in screw design and the higher engine speeds of compound engines, which eliminated the need for gearing, eventually tilted the balance in favour of the propeller, and Brunel's decisions, taken almost a generation earlier, were vindicated.

It is unlikely that the significance of the *Great Britain,* as a 'landmark' in the history of naval architecture, was appreciated in an era of dynamic commercial development. Her owners periodically offered her for sale but there were no bidders even when the price was as low as £6,500. Eventually, in 1881, she passed into the hands of a Mr J. C. Hayne of 15 Bishopsgate, London EC2, and a Captain J. Morris was appointed in command. Her connection with Gibbs, Bright and Co was resumed the following year however when she came under the ownership of Antony Gibbs, Sons and Company. This company, also with headquarters in Bishopsgate, were in fact

The *Great Britain* as a sailing ship during the eighties. The hull had been sheathed with timber and her former machinery spaces were turned into extra cargo holds

successors to Gibbs, Bright and Company, so that the Bright family of Bristol and Liverpool retained their interest in the vessel more or less during the entire length of her varied career.

A change of ownership once more signalled drastic alterations. She was taken to the yard of H. & C. Grayson Ltd at Birkenhead, and converted into a fully rigged sailing ship. Her engines and boilers were taken out, and for some inexplicable reason her iron hull was sheathed with wood. The removal of the machinery reduced her tonnage to 2735 gross tons but with the additional cargo capacity she could carry 3000 tons of a bulk commodity, such as coal or grain. It was the intention of her new owners to employ her purely as a cargo vessel, operating to and from San Francisco round the Horn. Captain Henry Stap was appointed in command, and on 9 November 1882 she left Liverpool on her first voyage under sail alone. It was not an auspicious beginning for she had to return to Liverpool on the 24th of that month to repair a number of leaks. After a survey she was permitted to sail on 2 December, but on 30 January 1883 she had to put into Montevideo, as the crew refused to proceed any further unless she was lightened and the cargo restowed. Some 500 tons were taken from the lower hold and stowed between decks, while a further 200 tons were unloaded ashore. Eventually she arrived at San Francisco on 2 June 1883, the voyage from Liverpool having taken just over six months. After spending most of the summer in San Francisco, she left on the homeward journey on 30 August with a cargo of wheat. She called at Cork for orders before proceeding to Liverpool to discharge. The second voyage was slightly quicker but followed the pattern of the first— Liverpool to San Francisco via the Horn and back to Cork with wheat and then on to Liverpool; this was completed on 12 July 1885. There was a long interval before the next voyage, and it is probable that her owners experienced difficulty in finding cargoes for a ship that was then forty years old. She eventually sailed from Penarth in February 1886 with a cargo of coal for Panama. This again entailed sailing round the Horn where she met very heavy weather and was partly dismasted as well as sustaining other structural damage. She returned to Port Stanley in the Falkland Islands for repairs, arriving there on 25 May 1886. A survey was made of the damage and, in view of the lack of facilities for carrying out major repairs, it was decided to abandon her as a hulk. The active career of the *Great Britain* was over.

6 · The Great Britain comes Home

Although she was patently unseaworthy the *Great Britain* continued to perform a useful service. She passed into the hands of the Falkland Islands Company who used her for over forty years as a store for coal and for the seasonal wool clip. She remained afloat in Port Stanley harbour during this period, and an eye witness has described how she was a familiar sight from the sea wall swinging at anchor in accordance with the wind and tide. Her new owners adapted her slightly for their purpose. Most of her internal fittings were stripped and, slightly forward of midships on the starboard side, a large hole was cut near the main deck to facilitate the stowage of wool. The South Atlantic weather—sun, wind, rain and incessant salt spray—gradually took its toll and by 1933 she was unserviceable, even as a wool store.

Various schemes were considered for her disposal, such as filling her with rubble and incorporating her into a jetty, or towing her up one of the numerous creeks of the main island where she could be sunk and used as the foundations of a bridge. The latter, however, was found to be impracticable on account of her draught. In 1936, the first positive plans were made to salvage the *Great Britain*. The Governor of the Falkland Islands at the time, Sir Henniker Heaton, decided to launch an appeal through the columns of *The Times* for the necessary funds and the Falkland Islands Company offered, in the event of a satisfactory response, to present the ship to the British Government. With a nice sense of timing, it was decided to open the appeal on 25 May 1936—the fiftieth anniversary of the end of her last voyage. A preliminary survey, however, showed that the salvage operations would then cost over £10,000 and the project was abandoned. Almost in despair she was offered to the Admiralty as a gunnery target but fortunately for posterity the offer was declined—perhaps out of respect for her age and history.

In 1937, the Falkland Islands Company decided to place her in honourable retirement at Sparrow Cove about four miles from Port Stanley on the north side of the outer harbour of Port William.

Beached in Sparrow Cove—her home for thirty-three years

She was towed there on 14 April, and deliberately holed for the second time in her long career to ensure that she rested firmly on the sea bed. Because of the scarcity of timber on the islands, some of her decking was removed and used for various projects at Port Stanley.

Otherwise she was left unattended and in due course the ravages of the South Atlantic storms began to cause even more serious deterioration of the hull structure. The two holes cut in her stern when she was beached allowed the interior to gradually silt up, and in some places the iron plates of the hull corroded to such an extent that it was nearly possible to see daylight through them. One visitor had the impression that in certain areas it was only the wooden sheathing that held the hull together. The most serious example of deterioration was a crack which appeared on the starboard side at the bottom of the hole cut to facilitate the loading of wool. As time passed this extended almost to the waterline and the strain exerted on this part of the ship was so severe during rough weather that the stout outer wooden sheathing was splintered at this point. This accentuated the plight of the vessel and a number of observers gloomily predicted that, if left unchecked, the crack would eventually cause her to break her back.

Many visitors to the Falklands—especially those with sea-going connections—made the pilgrimage to Sparrow Cove to witness the sad decay of the *Great Britain,* and from time to time reports of her condition filtered back to maritime societies and other interested

A close up of the bow. Part of the Royal Coat of Arms is still in position. The wooden sheathing added during 1881–2 did not extend to the tip of the bow and the original clinker-built hull can still be seen. The ironwork here is in remarkably good condition

bodies in Britain and the USA. During the mid-1960s the Society for Nautical Research planned a comprehensive photographic survey to record for posterity the last days of this unique vessel. At that time there was a general upsurge in interest in industrial archeology and also in the restoration of ships of special merit. Public interest in vessels such as the *Cutty Sark* in Britain and the *Vasa* in Sweden was encouraging, and so after an interval of over thirty years the question of salvaging the *Great Britain* was once again considered.

Like so many projects depending for success on the initiative and co-operation of a group of like-minded individuals, the operation began with a letter to *The Times*. The writer was Dr E. C. B. Corlett, a naval architect, who for many years had been carrying out a thorough investigation into the design and construction of the vessel. Dr Corlett's letter, which appeared in *The Times* on 11 November 1967, read as follows

Sir,
    The first iron-built ocean-going steamship and the first such ship to be driven entirely by a propeller was the *Great Britain*, designed and launched by Isambard Kingdom Brunel. This, the forefather of all modern ships, is lying a beached hulk in the Falkland Islands at this moment.
    The *Cutty Sark* has rightly been preserved at Greenwich and H.M.S. *Victory* at Portsmouth. Historically the *Great Britain* has an equal claim to fame and yet nothing has been done to document the hulk, let alone recover it and preserve it for record.
    May I make a plea that the authorities should at least document, photograph and fully record this wreck and at best do something to recover the ship and place her on display as one of the very few really historic ships still in existence.
                    Yours faithfully
                    E. C. B. Corlett

The main deck showing considerable signs of deterioration after over eighty years in the Falkland Islands

The crack on the starboard side which spread from the rectangular hole cut in the hull during her service as a wool store. This picture was taken during pumping out at the beginning of the salvage operations

Within ten days of publication several other letters appeared, notably from the Chairman of the Falkland Islands Company in London and from the Secretary of the Society for Nautical Research. The latter disclosed that there was a move afoot by the San Francisco Maritime Museum to purchase the hulk, which was now officially a Crown Wreck, and tow it to the USA for preservation. This caused much heart-searching in nautical circles in Britain and a committee was formed under the chairmanship of Mr Richard Goold-Adams to investigate the possibilities of bringing the *Great Britain* back to the country in which she was built. Finance was a major problem and the committee was under no illusions regarding the expense of the operation. When an appeal was launched however it evoked an amazing response and mainly through the generosity of one man, Mr Jack Haywood who donated £150,000, sufficient money was quickly raised to cover the anticipated costs of the salvage operations. The San Francisco Maritime Museum magnanimously agreed to withdraw their own plans and offered the project committee considerable assistance. The British Government also took a hand and enabled Dr Corlett to visit the Falkland Islands in November 1968 to make a thorough survey of the vessel. With the aid of a party from HMS *Endurance,* which included a team of divers, he reported that salvage of the *Great Britain* would be entirely feasible and that repairs should not be a serious problem. He concluded that the whole task of salvage should be within the competence of an efficient tug and crew although he warned that there was not unlimited time. The crack on the starboard side would open with gathering speed if no action was taken and eventually she would split in two.

The original plan was to tow the *Great Britain* back across the Atlantic, but Corlett advised against this, and it was decided instead to transport the hull on a submersible pontoon. A contract for the salvage operation was awarded to the Anglo-German consortium of Risdon Beazley of Southampton, and Ulrich Harms of Hamburg. All through 1969, a close watch was kept on the notorious crack which was now 8in wide in parts and there were many anxious moments for the Falkland Island representative of the project committee, Mr John Smith. In December 1969, he telephoned Dr Corlett in Britain to report that the massive main mast had tilted in a gale. Had the mast fallen, it would have probably crashed through the rotting deck timbers and ended all question of salvage. At no little risk to himself and with the aid of a local fisherman, John Smith managed to hammer wedges around the base of the mast to correct the tilt, and at the same time he stopped the heavy yard from swinging free in the wind. This was only a temporary expedient but it helped to prevent any further damage being sustained until the salvage flotilla arrived in Port Stanley on 25 March 1970.

Meanwhile negotiations with the Foreign and Commonwealth Office for the transfer of ownership were opened in London by the Project Committee. Public opinion in the Falklands was sounded, and it was apparent that the majority of the islanders felt that the rightful home of the *Great Britain* was in the United Kingdom, although there were many who gave the venture little chance of success. A few saw the ship as a tourist attraction and said that the hulk should not leave, while one influential islander considered that the money to be spent on the salvage could be better employed in helping to meet the cost of a much-needed airstrip. But despite these reservations, the islanders received the salvage flotilla with their traditional courtesy and hospitality.

The flotilla consisted of the tug *Varius II,* 724 tons, commanded by Captain Hans Hertzog with a crew of fifteen, and the submersible pontoon *Mulus III* with a displacement of 2667 tons. The tug and pontoon had just previously completed an assignment in Guinea, West Africa from whence they sailed across the South

Atlantic to Montevideo. It was here that a number of key personnel, including Leslie O'Neil, the senior salvage expert of the consortium with a team of four divers, and Horst Kaulen from Hamburg, a specialist in operations involving submersible pontoons, joined the salvage team.

Salvage operations began almost immediately after the arrival in Port Stanley. The tug and pontoon proceeded to Sparrow Cove and moored alongside the *Great Britain*. The divers were soon busy patching the holes in the hull with plywood and concrete, but the large crack on the starboard side was less easy to repair. Eventually a variation of an age-old seaman's method of dealing with leaks was adopted. But, instead of using hammocks to fill the gap, an appeal was made to the people of Port Stanley which brought forth a supply of old foam rubber and kapok matresses. These were forced into the crack where it extended below the waterline and held in place with plywood. Massive steel plates were then fixed in position to ensure watertightness when the ship was refloated once more.

The responsibility of removing the masts fell to Horst Kaulen. This was a major task but the operation was completed in less than a week with the aid of a crane erected on the pontoon. It was decided to remove the mizzen first. This was cut off below the level of the upper deck, but an accident occurred when it was being lifted out by the crane. A rotten section in the lower end broke, and the rest fell from about 15ft, crashing through the remains of the deckhouse. Fortunately, nobody was hurt, but Kaulen decided to cut the other masts above the deck level to make the operation easier. Previously, the yard on the main mast, which must have been one of the largest ever fitted on a sailing vessel, had been removed. After this, the fore and main masts presented relatively little difficulty. They were cut near the base and wedges were hammered in to tilt them over. These two masts were secured to the pontoon for towing back with the hull but the mizzen was handed over to the islanders to commemorate the years spent by the *Great Britain* in the Falklands.

The most critical stage in the operation began at midnight on 6 April when the diving team began pumping out the flooded hull with four pumps having a total capacity of 660 tons per hour. By the following morning, more than 2000 tons of water had been removed and the *Great Britain* was afloat for the first time in 33 years. Bad weather, with gusty 30 knot winds halted further progress until 10 April, and the salvage crews were hard put to prevent the ship from breaking away. As soon as the winds died down, the pontoon was submerged and with the aid of an additional tug—

An aerial view of the salvage operations. The tug *Varius II* and the submersible pontoon *Mulus III* are alongside the hulk, the three masts have been removed and pumping out is in progress

Proceeding up the Bristol Channel towards the end of one of the longest tows in maritime history. The hulk is firmly secured between a number of steel tubes welded to the deck of the pontoon

the *Lively,* owned by the Falkland Islands Company—the *Great Britain* was towed over the pontoon. A series of steel tubes had previously been welded to the deck of the pontoon so that the vessel could be accurately manoeuvred into position. This had to be accomplished in two stages. At the first attempt she grounded during the last 25ft of the tow but on the next evening tide it was possible to locate her exactly as required. As the tide ebbed later that night the ship began to settle down on the pontoon and the crack on the starboard side closed up causing the steel backing plate to buckle. Happily it had performed its allotted task and its failure at this stage was of no consequence. The pumping out of the pontoon took about 24 hours. Inch by inch the *Great Britain* emerged from the water until the graceful outline of Patterson's hull was visible at a glance. She was secured firmly in position and on 14 April was towed from Sparrow Cove to Port Stanley flying the Falkland Islands' ensign.

Her return to Stanley was treated as a gala event and her arrival in the harbour was signalled by ships' sirens. the bells of Christchurch Cathedral and the horns of almost every car on the island.

A few days later at a simple ceremony the Governor, Sir Cosmo Haskard, officially transferred the ownership to the Project Committee. Another week was spent in wiring and welding her even more firmly to the pontoon, and further attention was given to the crack on the starboard side, since she would need to be watertight for the last stage of her journey up the Avon. It was a poignant moment for the islanders as she finally left on 24 April, on what the Project Committee referred to as 'voyage 47'—a code name selected because it was on her forty-seventh voyage from Penarth in 1886 that she had sought refuge in the Falklands.

Two masterpieces by Brunel. The *Great Britain* passing beneath the Clifton Suspension Bridge on her journey up the River Avon on Sunday 5 July 1970

For the salvage crew, the first few hours were critical, as nobody was really certain how she would react once at sea. They were met with a force eight wind, but the ship and pontoon gave no trouble, and the first leg of the journey to Montevideo proceeded smoothly. Altogether the main leg of the 9000 mile tow back to Bristol took 49 days at an average speed of just over 5 knots. The only other period of bad weather occurred off the Canary Islands when adverse winds reduced their progress to 40 miles in 24 hours. Afterwards the convoy was able to make up time, and finally arrived off the mouth of the Avon on 22 June, only a day later than their estimated time of arrival. The hull was then removed from the pontoon with aid of two Bristol tugs, and a few minor repairs were made in the Avonmouth Docks prior to her passage up river.

The day originally chosen for the triumphant return to Bristol was Saturday 4 July, to take advantage of the spring tide. But the wind was too high that evening and the attempt was postponed for twelve hours. The final stage was not without drama. With one tug at her bow and one at her stern she left her moorings at 6.35 am on Sunday morning, and after heading out to sea swung round to enter the mouth of the river. About 30 minutes later, one of the steel hawsers from the leading tug parted, but prompt action by the crew kept the *Great Britain* under control and another hawser was quickly put on board. The last days of the tow from the Falklands had been fully covered in the press and by television cameras, but the nine-mile journey up the Avon was the first opportunity

The triumphant return to Bristol. Negotiating the locks was still a tricky manoeuvre but this time the masonry remained intact

afforded to the general public of seeing Brunel's ship at close quarters. They came in their thousands to cheer. Every vantage point along the river was crowded and car horns added to the cacophany of sound which must have exceeded even the noise at her launching on another July day, over a century and a quarter earlier. Perhaps the most spectacular view was obtained by those on or near the Clifton Suspension Bridge—another of Brunel's masterpieces which had been designed but not completed when the *Great Britain* sped seawards in 1844, after her enforced captivity in the Floating Harbour.

The return passage through the locks and into the Cumberland Basin still required careful handling, although the opening was several feet wider than when Brunel and Patterson removed the masonry on that dark December day. This time there were a few feet to spare. The Bristol-based tug *John King* then took over the bow-tow, and the City Dock pilots assumed responsibility for the final phase of the operation. She eventually moved into the Float at 10.30 am to the accompaniment of a rising crescendo of cheers and ships' sirens. The journey was almost over. At the end of St Augustine's Reach she was swung round and slowly berthed at 'Y' shed

Moving into the heart of Bristol, the *Great Britain* returns to the city which she had left a hundred and twenty-six years earlier

where the Lord Mayor of Bristol and other civic leaders were waiting to welcome her. The *Great Britain* had come home.

The last act took place on 19 July 1970, exactly 127 years after her launch by the Prince Consort. By happy coincidence the highest spring tide of the month was expected on that day. Even so, it was hardly sufficient to float her back into the Wapping Dock where she had been built, and action was taken to raise her stern to give her a draught of 13ft. She was eased into place almost inch by inch during the evening, the operation being watched by millions of television viewers as well as thousands on the dockside.

And so ended one of the most difficult and complex salvage operations in maritime history. But for the *Great Britain* it was the end and the beginning. It is planned to restore her externally to the form of the original Brunel ship. The first set of engines will be reproduced complete with the chain drive and propeller shaft, and

Shortly after her return the vessel was opened to the public and the Project Committee reported 12,000 visitors during the first five days

a portion of the interior will be restored to show typical cabins and a saloon of the period. A large area however will be reserved for a modern technological display centre—a wise decision, and one which surely would have met with the approval of her original building committee Brunel, Claxton and Guppy—who with William Patterson conceived and built 'the great iron ship' that changed the course of ship development a century and a quarter ago.

Appendixes

APPENDIX ONE

Principal dimensions of the ss *Great Britain* (as completed in 1844).

Length (stem to stern)	322ft
Length (keel)	289ft
Maximum beam	50ft 6in
Depth of hold	32ft 6in
Draught	16ft
Gross tonnage	2936 tons
Net tonnage	1017 tons
Passenger capacity	360
Cargo capacity	1000 tons
Coal in bunkers	1000 tons
Power	1000 nhp
Weight of iron in hull	1040 tons
Weight of engines and boilers	520 tons

APPENDIX TWO

Building Costs (as incurred by the Great Western Steamship Company 1838-1844).

	£	s	d
Total cost of vessel	117,295	6	7
Building establishment	53,081	12	9
Alterations to locks	1,330	4	9
Hull, engines and boilers	73,000	0	0
Fittings, rigging and stores	18,000	0	0
Rents, interest charges	26,000	0	0

(Reprinted from *The Steamship Great Britain*
by G. Farr, Bristol, 1965)

APPENDIX THREE

Statement of Accounts on Winding Up of Great Western Steamship Company 28 January 1852.

Profit and Loss 1st December 1851

	£ s. d.	£ s. d.	£ s. d.		£ s. d.	£ s. d.
To Balance 31st Decr 1850	153 8 0			By Shareholders for 1794 ordinary shares of £100 ea. written off as total loss, these having been paid thereon only		179,300 5 4
Coal Shed at Liverpool	66 10 0			£43,005 12 5		
Less sale of Stores		86 18 0				
Great Britain balance 31. 12. 1850	125,555 5 1			Balance carried down		
Less sale after deducting Expenses comm etc	17,658 17 11		107,896 7 2			
Works balance 31. 12. 1850	49,529 14 3					
Less sale after expenses etc	2,246 13 6		47,277 0 11			
General Expenditure. Office expenses, Stamps, Salary and a/c not previously sent in previously sent in		304 10 3				
Dr Secretary for Salary which had remained in obeyance from July 1844 to 31st Decr 1849 as agreed		400 0 0				
Osborne overcharged on Iron etc		7 5 0				
	155,972 2 1					
Less Interest deducted from new shares in arrears	116 17 2				155,855 4 11	
					198,860 17 4	£198,860 17 4
Balance brought down					£19560 12 0	

Resting Balances 1st Decr 1851

Dr

	£	s.	d.	£	s.	d.
Profit and Loss for Balance				19,560	12	0
Office furniture	128	19	4			
R. Irvin, New York balance of a/c still left open, on a/c of Debenture on Coal claimable from the Government of United States. It is possible that ultimately something more may be recovered from that source	201	2	11			
Gibbs, Bright & Co Liverpool balance	3	14	6			
Miles and Co Bankers balance	422	5	2	333	16	9
Cash ditto	28	10	9			
				450	15	11
				£20,345	4	8

Cr

	£	s.	d.
Shareholder for balance of new or £30 shares	20,319	17	2
Dividends unclaimed	25	7	6

Vouched and examined
John Moxham, Public Accountant

Bristol 24th Dec 1851

Bibliography

Brunel, I. K. jun., *The Life of Isambard Kingdom Brunel*, 1870

Claxton, C., *The Great Britain Steam Ship*, 1847

Daniel, H., 'The Great Britain', *J. Hon. Co. Master Mariners*, 1, 1935, 245-9

Farr, G., *The Steamship Great Britain*, Bristol, 1965

Grantham, J., *Iron as a Material for Shipbuilding*, Liverpool, 1842

Guppy, T. R. *Proceedings*, Institution of Civil Engineers, 4, 1845, 151-85

Hopkinson, J., *The Working of the Steam Engine Explained*, 1857

Hudson, K., *Industrial Archaeology of Southern England*, Newton Abbot, 1968

Inkster, W. S., *Captain John Gray*, The New Shetlander, 81, 1967, 14-16

Millar, J., 'The Invasion of 1854', *Melbourne Quarterly*, 14, 1963, 32-7

Noble, C. B., *The Brunels, Father and Son*, 1938

Rees, H., *British Ports and Shipping*, 1958

Rolt, L. T. C., *Isambard Kingdom Brunel*, 1961

Rowland, K. T., *Steam at Sea*, Newton Abbot, 1970

Spratt, H. Philip, *Marine Engineering* (Science Museum Catalogue Part II, 1953)

Spratt, H. Philip, *Outline History of Transatlantic Steam Navigation*, 1950

Tute, W., *Atlantic Conquest*, 1816-1961, 1961

Weale, J., *The Great Britain Atlantic Steam Ship*, 1847

Index

Since numerous alterations were made to the *Great Britain* during her long career references to the ship as completed in 1844 are not dated in the index. Subsequent changes in structure are indicated with the date in brackets.